THE GRAND TRAVERSE OF THE MASSIF CENTRAL

BY MOUNTAIN BIKE, ROAD BIKE OR ON FOOT

Ala..orth and South Am......., ...years led organised walking holidays in several European countries. A member of the British Outdoor Writers and Photographers Guild, he has written more than a dozen guidebooks, several on long-distance mountain routes in France. His longer solo walks include a *grand traverse* of the European Alps between Nice and Vienna (2430km/1510 miles), the Pilgrim's Trail from Le Puy to Santiago de Compostela (1545km/960 miles) and a coast-to-coast across the French Pyrenees (870km/540 miles). His cycle tours include Land's End to John O'Groats, and several long European rides in France, Germany, Austria, Belgium and Holland. A Munroist and erstwhile national secretary of the Long Distance Walkers Association, Alan now lives at the foot of the Moffat Hills in Scotland, in the heart of the Southern Uplands.

Alan has been exploring the French Massif Central for over 20 years, since his first visit to the Velay and Cévennes in 1988, to research the route taken by Robert Louis Stevenson a century earlier. He has walked many hundreds of miles of the region's trails, including the GR4, as well as circular tours of the Velay, Cévennes, Mont Lozère and Mont Aigoual, and long trails in the Causses. In addition to the Grand Traverse of the Massif Central (GTMC), Alan has also toured the Massif Central by bicycle as part of a 2400km (1500 mile) cycle tour around France.

Other Cicerone guidebooks by the author

Walks in Volcano Country
(Auvergne and Velay, France)
Walking the French Gorges
(Provence and the Ardèche)
The Brittany Coastal Path
Walking in the Ardennes

The River Rhine Trail
Walking in Bedfordshire
The John Muir Trail
The Southern Upland Way
The Robert Louis Stevenson Trail
The Tour of the Queyras

MRT 7/12

THE GRAND TRAVERSE OF THE MASSIF CENTRAL

BY MOUNTAIN BIKE, ROAD BIKE OR ON FOOT

by
Alan Castle

2 POLICE SQUARE, MILNTHORPE, CUMBRIA LA7 7PY
www.cicerone.co.uk

Acknowledgements

My wife, Beryl Castle, has always over the years given freely of her advice, support and encouragement during the planning, research and writing of my guidebooks, and for this book there was no exception. For this I am ever grateful. Beryl accompanied me on my ride across the Massif Central along the GTMC and has also helped in the preparation of the sketch maps for this guidebook. I am indebted to Alan and Sheila Sides, two experienced cyclists and mountain bikers, who accompanied us in France and offered much advice. In particular they provided plenty of information and suggestions for a road route across the region. Finally, I thank the team at Cicerone Press for their professionalism in publishing this and my other guidebooks.

Dedicated to all lovers of adventure and to Carys – may she enjoy life to the full.

'All I seek, the heaven above
And the road below me.'
'The Vagabond' from *Songs of Travel*, Robert Louis Stevenson, 1896

Front cover: Mountain bikers taking a break before the Buron de Paillassère–Bas (Stage 4, photo: Alan Sides)

CONTENTS

Map Key

D16 A71 N89 ▬▬▬	road	◎	puy
→	GTMC or Road Bike Route (depending on map)	▲	other peak
••••••••	other GR route (not followed)	✳ †	viewpoint
••••••••	alternative route	•	spot height
▬▬▬	route passing through national park	✦	monument
┼┼┼┼┼┼	railway	■	building
〜〜〜	river	◉	village/hamlet
◯	lake	▦	built-up area
→	direction arrow	⌒	bridge

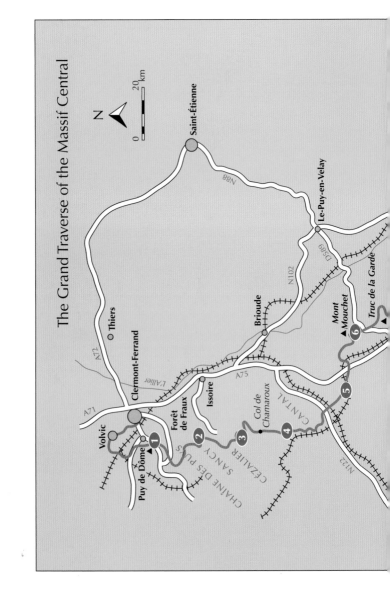

The Grand Traverse of the Massif Central

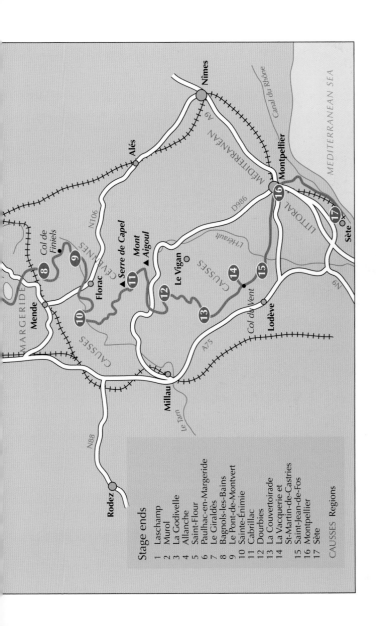

Stage ends

1 Laschamp
2 Murol
3 La Godivelle
4 Allanche
5 Saint-Flour
6 Paulhac-en-Margeride
7 Le Giraldès
8 Bagnols-les-Bains
9 Le Pont-de-Montvert
10 Sainte-Énimie
11 Cabrillac
12 Dourbies
13 La Couvertoirade
14 La Vacquerie et
    St-Martin-de-Castries
15 Saint-Jean-de-Fos
16 Montpellier
17 Sète

CAUSSES Regions

A narrow street in Ispagnac (Stage 10)

ROUTE SUMMARY TABLE

		Distance (km)	Distance (miles)	Distance from start/to end of GTMC (km)	Ascent/descent (m)	% of stage off-road
STAGE 1	Clermont-Ferrand to Laschamp	56.0	34.8	56/662	934/490	71
STAGE 2	Laschamp to Murol	47.0	29.2	103/615	660/760	74
STAGE 3	Murol to La Godivelle	34.0	21.1	137/581	821/336	73
STAGE 4	La Godivelle to Allanche	30.5	18.9	167.5/550.5	283/558	33
STAGE 5	Allanche to Saint-Flour	42.0	26.1	209.5/508.5	496/636	52
STAGE 6	Saint-Flour to Paulhac-en-Margeride	43.0	26.7	252.5/465.5	1002/638	69
STAGE 7	Paulhac-en-Margeride to Le Giraldés	52.7	32.7	305.2/412.8	825/598	80
STAGE 8	Le Giraldés to Bagnols-les-Bains	35.8	22.2	341/377	240/640	81
STAGE 9	Bagnols-les-Bains to Le Pont-de-Montvert	44.3	27.5	385.3/332.7	760/740	64
STAGE 10	Le Pont-de-Montvert to Sainte-Énimie	53.7	33.4	439/279	477/726	44
STAGE 11	Sainte-Énimie to Cabrillac	38.7	24.0	477.7/240.3	991/428	23
STAGE 12	Cabrillac to Dourbies	49.5	30.7	527.2/190.8	895/1185	64
STAGE 13	Dourbies to La Couvertoirade	44.7	27.8	571.9/146.1	758/818	56
STAGE 14	La Couvertoirade to La Vacquerie et St-Martin-de-Castries	31.1	19.3	603/115	263/415	75
STAGE 15	La Vacquerie et St-Martin-de-Castries to Saint-Jean-de-Fos	37.5	23.3	640.5/77.5	620/1030	59
STAGE 16	Saint-Jean-de-Fos to Montpellier	39.5	24.5	680/38	266/400	39
STAGE 17	Montpellier to Sète	38.0	23.6	718/0	0/0	63
TOTAL	Clermont-Ferrand to Sète	718.0	446.0	–	10,291/10,398	60

INTRODUCTION

A LONG DISTANCE MOUNTAIN BIKE TRAIL

The GTMC (full title 'Grande Traversée du Massif Central' in French) is a long-distance mountain bike trail in France that crosses the huge, largely remote area of mountain, high plateaux, forests and heathland known as the Massif Central. This region stretches from almost the very centre of the country right down to the south at the Mediterranean coast, a total area of some 93,000km² (36,000 square miles). The trail runs for 718km (446 miles), from the large city of Clermont-Ferrand in the heart of France to the town of Sète, south of Montpellier on the Mediterranean.

Developed by the outdoor organisation Chamina and the FFC (Fédération Française de Cyclisme), the GTMC was the first long-distance mountain bike trail to be completed in France. There are now several other such trails, known as VTT routes ('Vélo Tout Terrain', or all-terrain bicycle, in other words 'mountain bike'), in areas such as the Pyrenees and Alps, but the GTMC remains one of the most popular, rewarding and challenging long-distance bike trails in France. It may particularly appeal to British mountain bikers, as there are no similar long-distance routes designed for mountain bikers in the UK, only multi-user routes such as the South Downs Way and the Pennine Bridleway.

A good cycling track (Stage 3)

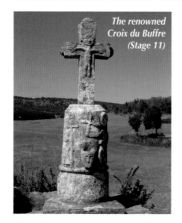

The renowned Croix du Buffre (Stage 11)

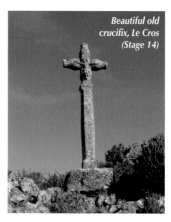

Beautiful old crucifix, Le Cros (Stage 14)

Christ washing the disciples' feet, Clermont-Ferrand (Stage 1)

Ancient cross at Le Viallard (Stage 1)

La Croix de Mâitre-Vidal (Stage 9)

Most of the road sections of the route are along minor rural roads and lanes, with little passing traffic, although there are occasional stretches along busier roads. However, around 60 per cent of the GTMC is off-road on a variety of surfaces, from wide forest gravel roads to narrow muddy woodland tracks, from gentle, smooth paths to quite fierce ascents and descents on some very rough terrain, often exacerbated by tree roots, rocks and stones.

The majority of the route does not require any highly technical mountain biking skill, just concentration, care and common sense. Some relatively small sections are difficult and somewhat technical, but these can either be fairly easily avoided altogether by taking an alternative route, or the difficulties considerably reduced by simply dismounting and pushing your bike. Never hesitate to do this if you are unsure of your ability to safely negotiate a section, and if you are still unsure even about pushing, go back to the nearest road and rejoin the route of the GTMC later.

A lot will depend on weather conditions, not only at the time of your visit, but in the preceding weeks, as lots of heavy rain can quickly turn relatively firm tracks into quagmires of mud. Beneath a canopy of trees where the sun is unable to penetrate, the rate of drying of rain-soaked tracks and paths will be much slower than in open countryside. Generally, the further south you are, the fewer muddy

tracks you are likely to encounter, as the warmer Mediterranean climate gradually replaces the wetter, more temperate climate of the northern Massif Central.

Planning the schedule

The official guide to the GTMC (see Appendix C, Further Reading) gives a completion time for the full route of between 10 and 20 days. This wide range allows for the differences between, for example, fit and expert mountain bikers, perhaps with a support back-up vehicle, who wish to make rapid progress along the trail, relative beginners, and/or those who prefer to take their time, visiting various places of interest along the way, and if unsupported, who need time to find accommodation and buy supplies.

This guidebook divides the GTMC into 17 stages, each of which the average mountain biker should accomplish in a day. The stages are, however, easy to adjust, as in most areas there are other accommodation possibilities, which allow the cyclist to split his or her days as required.

Those who wish to sample only a section of the GTMC can do so by making use of the railway stations en route, the main ones of which are at Clermont-Ferrand, Neussargues, Saint-Flour, Montpellier and Sète. The GTMC can be split into two approximately equal halves by leaving or joining the route at Bagnols-les-Bains, the nearest main railway station to which is at the town of Mende, 20km by road from Bagnols, although there is a smaller station at the village of Allenc, 10km away.

GR trails and GR de Pays

The GTMC uses a variety of different designated routes, including a considerable number of *grandes randonnées* (or GR trails), which are well known to walkers of the French countryside. France has a very extensive network of these official long-distance paths (literally 'big walks'), each of which has a number, for example GR7 or GR65, and is waymarked with a system of red and white paint marks.

The principal long-distance trails usually carry a low number, for example GR4 or GR6, whereas shorter circular routes, variations or links have two- or three-digit numbers. Trails in the vicinity of a one-digit GR route all carry the same first

Waymarking for walkers and cyclists (Stage 1)

number. For example the GR4 has the associated GR43, 44 and 412; the GR6 has the associated GR60 and 65, and so on. This system has analogies with the road-numbering system in Britain: M6, M62, M606, and so on. A circular GR route is generally referred to as a 'tour', for example Tour des Cévennes, the GR67. There are at least 65,000km (approximately 40,000 miles) of GR trails throughout France and the network is still expanding.

In addition to the long-distance trails there are many usually shorter, regional footpaths, referred to as 'GR de Pays' (yellow and red waymarking), as well as a plethora of local footpaths, or 'Sentiers de PR' (petites randonnées), usually waymarked with yellow paint stripes.

In France the distinction between 'walkers only' footpaths, and bridleways for walkers, cyclists and horse riders, is less clear than it is in England and Wales. Many sections of the GR trails can be used by cyclists provided due consideration is given to other users. Trails for horse riders are waymarked with orange paint stripes, but these too often double up on GR trails. However, if a sign is encountered anywhere on the system prohibiting mountain bikes, then you must observe it.

The Route

The GTMC starts in the large industrial city of Clermont-Ferrand, but once it has bid farewell to this metropolis there are no more similarly

Typical village by the Tarn (Stage 10) (Alan Sides)

large urban areas until the elegant city of Montpellier, near the end of the journey. Farms, hamlets, villages large and small, and moderately sized towns connect this rural trail across some of the most scenic areas of the Massif Central.

Perversely, for a trail that is to head south to the coast, the GTMC begins by travelling north, to visit the town of Volvic, famed for its natural spring water. The fascinating visitor centre here should not be missed, before you continue across the Monts Dôme, an incredible area dotted with many long-extinct volcanoes, the highest of which is the Puy de Dôme, at 1464m (4800ft).

The next few days are spent in the Parc Naturel Régional des Volcans d'Auvergne, at first following the main

Chaîne des Puys of volcanic hills, and then skirting to the east of the Monts-Dore, a series of high peaks and ridges topped by the highest summit in the whole of the Massif Central, the Puy de Sancy (1886m/6186ft). The GTMC crosses the high Cézallier plateau and then to the east of the extinct Cantal volcanoes, before descending first to Allanche and then to the historic town of Saint-Flour.

The first stage of the GTMC now over, the route then proceeds over the high hills of the Margeride, a remote area from which many Maquis operations were launched during the Second World War. The national monument to the French Resistance is located near the highest summit of the Margeride, Mont Mouchet, at 1490m (4887ft), and there is the opportunity to visit both. The way continues across sparsely populated country – passing the route taken since medieval times by pilgrims travelling to Santiago de Compostela in northwest Spain – finally descending to the spa town of Bagnols-les-Bains.

The trail now stands at the northern foot of the Cévennes, one of southern France's most romantically beautiful areas. The crossing of this great range of high, forested hills begins with a traverse of Mont Lozère, beneath the summit of its highest mountain, the Pic de Finiels (1699m/5570ft), before a long descent to Le Pont-de-Montvert.

This charming village, steeped in history, lies on the River Tarn, perhaps southern France's most celebrated river. More Cévenol hills are traversed as the GTMC now heads west, over the Bougès ridge to Florac, capital of the Cévennes, where the Tarn is encountered once more. We are now close to some of the spectacular Tarn Gorges, above which our trail journeys still westwards to reach one of the main settlements on the river, Sainte-Énimie, ancient village turned water sports capital.

The Tarn is reluctantly left behind as the trail crosses the sun-baked and often windswept Causse Méjean, a very extensive high limestone plateau, ablaze with flowers in the springtime. The southern Cévennes then have to be conquered, the GTMC climbing to its very highest point, the summit of Mont Aigoual, an extensive viewpoint. The

Trèvezel Gorges are passed en route for an overnight at the *gîte d'étape* at the picturesque village of Dourbies. A final climb over the southernmost of the Cévennes hills and forests leads to a lower, more open plain, which is crossed to reach the historic, small walled town of La Couvertoirade, another grand place to spend the night.

Our trail continues across more fairly open plain, dotted with tiny settlements, until the foot of the last major barrier before the coastal plain is reached. The crossing of the high Saint-Baudille range of limestone hills, and a visit to the revered village of Saint-Guilhem-le-Désert in the l'Hérault valley, are both highlights of the next stage. Only a visit to refined Montpellier remains before the Mediterranean Sea is reached, for a very relaxing finale to the GTMC – a ride or walk along the Canal du Rhône to journey's end, the 'island' peninsula that is the town of Sète.

A GTMC FOR ROAD CYCLISTS

A traverse of the Massif Central, following the line of the GTMC very approximately, can also be made by road cyclists. This visits all the major places through which the GTMC passes, but keeps to roads – for the most part relatively quiet ones, where the volume of traffic is not excessive. There are several alternative routes, with the major contenders described in this guidebook. Such a road route would probably take the average cyclist somewhere between eight and 12 days, and would vary in distance between about 660km (410 miles) and 800km (500 miles), depending on the exact route chosen.

Mountain bikers need not always stick to the GTMC on their journey south, of course – you can easily 'mix and match', riding some sections of the GTMC and others on quiet roads. This option will probably appeal particularly to the less competent or enthusiastic mountain biker, especially in poor weather conditions (always remember that enjoyment is the main reason for making this journey).

WALKING THE GTMC

The GTMC not only makes an excellent off-road mountain bike trail across the hills, forests, plateaux and valleys of the Massif Central, but as such a high percentage of it is off-road, and much of that along numerous GR Trails, it also provides a first-rate long-distance walking route across the region. Rather like a coast-to-coast route in Britain, there is a great deal of satisfaction to be had from a project that involves traversing a whole region right down to the very edge of the sea.

The walking is generally straightforward, suitable for most reasonably fit people, and the terrain mainly easy going, although there is naturally

Leaving Saint-Guilhem-le-Désert (Stage 15) (Alan Sides)

considerable ascent and descent along the course of the entire route. Fast progress can often be made, particularly along sections of quiet lane and firm tracks.

Although the GTMC is intended as a mountain bike trail, many walkers use it as well, particularly along the frequent and lengthy sections that coincide with GR trails. You will encounter relatively few cyclists, rarely more than two or three each day, and nearly all of these are highly respectful of other trail users. Information for those walking the trail is included in this guidebook, at the end of each stage, and alternatives are given where the GTMC trail can be left for other routes and later rejoined, particularly in areas where there is a considerable amount of road walking.

A walking traverse of the Massif Central would take the average long-distance walker from 27 to 32 days, so a four or five week trip from home, including travel to and from the region. Alternatively, the railway network easily allows one-, two- or three-week walking holidays to be planned.

CLIMATE – WHEN TO GO

In general terms, summers in the Massif Central tend to be hot and relatively dry, while winters are often cold with heavy snowfalls.

Winter (defined here as the beginning of November until the end of April) is definitely not a recommended season for travelling the GTMC, most

particularly by mountain bike, as snow and ice on the route would create very hazardous conditions, particularly on steep and rough sections. Temperatures are generally very low in wintertime, particularly along the higher sections of the trail away from the coast, and walkers also would require considerable experience. Even the road cyclist would face difficulties, with black ice and snow-blocked high sections on untreated minor roads. Moreover, hotel and other accommodation would probably pose quite a problem during winter, as many of the establishments along the trail close during this season.

The other three seasons all have their charms and advantages and disadvantages. Summer is undoubtedly the most popular season, although it does have its problems. Firstly, it can become intensely hot during the daytime in July and August, and care must be taken to avoid sunstroke and dehydration. Secondly, finding accommodation for each night will be more of a problem in summer (see Accommodation, below).

Springtime, with its flowers and freshness (May/June), is recommended, as is autumn (September/October), when the golden-brown tints of turning leaves can be particularly beautiful – chestnuts are everywhere on the ground, mushrooms of every size and hue abound in the forests, and the hedgerows are ripe with abundant fruits. The temperature can be quite low both early and late in the year, however, and weather conditions can change dramatically. Much of the trail lies at or above the 1000m (3278ft) contour, so temperatures can also drop rapidly. Late-lying snow on the high sections of the route in early May, and early falling snow in late October, are real possibilities.

Violent thunderstorms, often with little warning of their approach, are not uncommon at any time of year, particularly after the heat of a summer's afternoon, and are a particular hazard to be taken seriously (if such storms become frequent during hot afternoons, then start and finish the day early, to reduce the risk of being caught out in one).

SUPPORTED OR UNSUPPORTED

The majority of mountain bikers who tackle the GTMC do so without any support, carrying their equipment and finding their accommodation each day. The other way to ride the trail is to have a support vehicle and driver as back-up, and if someone will do this for you, there are distinct advantages.

The main advantage is that only a small amount of gear – food, drink, spare clothing, camera – need be carried, and this can be accommodated in a small backpack, so removing at a stroke the problem of carrying all the necessary equipment for the whole holiday on a bike that will be subjected to considerable jolting over the rough trail (see Equipment, below).

Typical Cévenol chestnut tree (Stage 10)

Also, the support person can find accommodation for each night while the mountain biker enjoys the riding, without having to think about finding somewhere to eat and rest for the night. The support person could spend the day sightseeing and meeting up with the rider from time to time. However, despite all the advantages of having support, the satisfaction and freedom of riding the GTMC unsupported is without parallel.

Road cyclists (who have smooth-surface riding) and walkers would have less advantage from a support team, unless camping, as the relatively small amount of gear necessary can easily be carried in either cycle panniers or a rucksack.

TRAVELLING TO AND FROM THE REGION

The easiest, quickest – and perhaps cheapest – way of travelling to the region is by aeroplane. Travelling to the Massif Central from the UK couldn't be easier these days, with several budget airlines offering inexpensive flights to Nîmes, Montpellier, Saint-Étienne, Lyon and Clermont-Ferrand, from Luton, Stansted and Heathrow in the southeast, from East Midlands, or from Liverpool and Prestwick, amongst others, in the north. There is usually an additional charge for transporting bicycles on budget airlines (and on some other carriers): the pedals must be taken off, handlebars straightened and secured,

and the bike packed in a bike box or bag for the journey. (When booking your first night's accommodation, it is a good idea to ask whether the proprietor will take care of the bike box or bag until your return for the flight home). For advice on transporting your bike on a plane, contact the CTC (see Appendix D, Useful Contacts).

The obvious airports are Clermont-Ferrand for the outward journey and Nîmes for the return. However, budget flights to Clermont-Ferrand from the UK are only from the London area, and do not operate every day. A good alternative is to fly both to and from Nîmes. At the time of writing, Ryanair is operating a daily return service to Nîmes from Luton, three times a week from East Midlands, and four times a week from Liverpool. The centre of Nîmes and its railway station is only 14km from the airport, an easy cycle ride of less than an hour (walkers can take the inexpensive airport bus that connects with all flights).

There are two or three non-TGV train services each day from Nîmes to Clermont-Ferrand, journey time approximately five hours. When purchasing your train ticket, do not forget to request a bicycle ticket (free of charge). There is usually little problem in transporting your bike, without dismantling it in any way, on normal express (non-TGV) and local trains in France, unless the train is very full, in which case you might be asked to take a later one. On finishing the GTMC, take a train from Sète via Montpellier

Sète railway station (Stage 17)

to Nîmes (frequent services, total journey time about 50 minutes).

If you don't want to fly, there are three other travel options: train from the UK to France, long-distance coach and private transport.

Eurostar services from London operate frequent daily trains to Paris, from where fast TGV and other trains leave for Clermont-Ferrand (but note that it will be necessary to change railway stations in Paris in order to continue on your journey). In general, you can only carry a bicycle at no extra charge on Eurostar if it is carried in a bike bag no larger than 120cm by 90cm, so the bike must be disassembled. However, there are two Eurostar services which do allow bikes to be

transported without dismantling, but for both these options you need a seat reservation first.

For the first option, you telephone the Eurostar Baggage Line on 0870 5850850 to book a bicycle reservation on your train (£20 per bike per journey in 2009). There are limited spaces for bicycles on each train, so it is advisable to make an early reservation. With this option you are assured that your bike will be travelling on the same train as you.

Alternatively, check in your bike at the Eurostar Baggage Office at the railway station up to one hour before your train departure. This service also costs £20, but there is no guarantee that you and your cycle will travel

23

on the same train. In this case, your bike will usually arrive a few hours after you, but Eurostar only guarantees that it will arrive within 24 hours after check-in, so at worst you could have to wait up to a day to retrieve your bicycle.

On most TGV services you will have to transport your bicycle in a bike bag no larger than 120 x 90cm, although a few TGV services now have a luggage van in which bikes can be transported without dismantling, for example on the Paris to Marseilles route. This service cost €10 per bike per journey in 2008. It may be that in the future this facility will be extended to other TGV routes – check the current situation and regulations on www.velo.sncf.com.

The *Express Bike Bus* is a company offering coach transport from England with bicycles towed in custom-built trailers. There are various pick-up points in England, including Leeds, Manchester, Birmingham, London and Dover. Their 'Mediterranean Route' service includes a drop-off near Montpellier. Services operate from early May to late September, with varying weekly/fortnightly departures and returns (see Appendix D, Useful Contacts).

There are several advantages of using a *private vehicle* to transport your bike to the Massif Central. Firstly, the bike does not need to be dismantled in any way, packed in a bike bag or box, nor re-assembled at journey's end, and you have total control at all

Sign for a typical gite

stages, remaining with your bicycle for the duration of the journey. You alone are responsible for securing your bike onto your vehicle, so that there are no concerns over possible damage by airport or train staff during handling, and no additional bike transport costs to pay. In addition, the use of private transport allows total flexibility over journey dates and timings.

The disadvantage, unless you have a vehicle back-up person or team, is that somewhere must be found for the safe storage of your car while on the GTMC. It is best to book a hotel or similar accommodation in advance for the first night, asking for your vehicle to be left in the establishment's car park for the duration of your holiday. (It is only reasonable, if the hotel grants this, to pay a reasonable daily parking fee, and to offer to stay a second night at the end of your trip before leaving for home.) The obvious place to drive to is Clermont-Ferrand. Leave your vehicle here and take a non-TGV train back with your bike from Sète/Montpellier at the end of your holiday.

ACCOMMODATION

Hotels, gîtes d'étape and chambres d'hôtes

Booking accommodation from the UK these days is relatively easy, thanks to the internet and e-mail. Some of the hotels and gîtes d'étape along the route now have websites, and enquiries and bookings are often possible by e-mail. Main tourist offices in the region (see Appendix D, Useful Contacts) will also send out lists of accommodation on request.

During the main summer season, and particularly between 14 July and 15 August (from Bastille Day to the Feast of the Assumption), many hotels and gîtes d'étape tend to be heavily booked, especially in the main tourist areas, so those intending to ride or walk the GTMC during July and August, or over French public holidays, are strongly advised to make reservations. At other times of year booking accommodation in advance may not be necessary, although it is always advisable, if possible, to phone for a booking one or two days ahead, particularly if you wish to take dinner on the evening when you arrive. If speaking French over the telephone is a problem for you, then either ask the proprietor of your current hotel or gîte d'étape to phone ahead for you, or ask the staff of a tourist office to do so. Most people are usually very willing to help.

Hotels in France are star graded according to a system very similar to that used in Britain. A basic hotel is a one-star establishment, and usually reasonably priced, clean and comfortable. Most of the hotels in the area covered by this guidebook carry a one- or two-star grading. One pays for the room in France, so there is seldom a reduction for only one occupant, although if cycling or walking alone it is always sensible to enquire.

The French gîte d'étape has similarities with the UK youth hostel, but is operated either privately (most are family-run small businesses) or by the local community (gîte communal). Many gîtes d'étape are in sympathetically restored traditional buildings, typically accommodating between 10 and 30 people. All have hot showers. Dinner is usually provided in a gîte d'étape and this nearly always consists of excellent home cooking, often to a much higher standard than that

Hotel de Paris in Murol (Stage 2)

Checking gear before leaving the gîte (Stage 8) (Alan Sides)

found in tourist restaurants. Most *gîtes d'étape* also have a fully equipped kitchen for those wishing to prepare their own food. Accommodation is in a traditional *dortoir*, usually of four, six or eight beds, but increasingly these days, rooms for two are also available at a little extra cost.

Demi-pensions are common and usually offer the best value for money. You will almost certainly meet other like-minded outdoor people here, usually walkers, mountain bikers or other cyclists, and these establishments are noted for their hospitality. Staying at a good *gîte d'étape* can be one of the highlights of walking or cycling in France. See Appendix

A for a list of the *gîtes d'étape* along the GTMC Trail. There is no umbrella organisation to join, but details of most of them can be found at www.gites-refuges.com.

Chambres d'hôtes are bed-and-breakfast establishments, similar to their British counterparts (although, of course, do not expect an English cooked breakfast). The cost always includes breakfast, but dinner is often not available, although it can usually be taken in a nearby restaurant. *Chambres d'hôtes* are becoming more and more popular in France, and to attract foreign guests will often be signposted as 'Bed & Breakfast', 'B&B', or '*zimmer-frei*'.

Camping

There are many campsites on or near the way – plentiful in some areas, but rather thin on the ground in others, particularly after Stage 13 until the coast is reached. For campers intending to ride or walk the GTMC late in the season, it is important to note that most campsites on the route close some time in September, often at the end of that month, but more than a few in the first or second week of September. If you intend to camp wild *(camping sauvage)* along the trail, be aware that you must seek permission from the landowner before doing so (it is illegal to do so otherwise). An uncontaminated water source will also have to be found, unless enough water is carried from a town or village. Leave no sign of an overnight camp, remove all your litter and take care not to pollute water sources. Particular care should be taken with matches and stoves, as forest fires are all too common during hot, dry summers, and do not light open fires. Note that wild camping is completely prohibited in the Cévennes National Park.

FOOD AND WATER

Shops, and in particular grocery shops *(épicerie)* and bakers *(boulangerie)*, tend to open earlier than their equivalents in Britain (usually around 7.30–8.00am) and to stay open later (often up to 8.00pm), but most will close for

The mobile butcher calls at Vacquerie-et-Saint-Martin-de-Castries (Stage 14)

two to three hours in the early afternoon (note that *boulangeries* often close earlier in the day, and rarely have fresh bread in the late afternoon). A few farms in some rural areas may offer items such as cheese or honey for sale, but never rely on this. Some smaller and more remote settlements, which no longer have village shops, are served by mobile shops that travel the district once, twice or three times a week, and you may just be lucky to encounter one. Provisions may sometimes be bought from the guardian of a *gîte d'étape*, who may also provide you with a packed lunch if you request it in advance.

Cyclists should carry water in frame-attached water-bottle carriers. There are water fountains in many of the villages and hamlets passed en route, and water bottles should always be filled when the opportunity arises. Daytime temperatures can be very high at times, particularly during July and August, and heat exhaustion and dehydration can develop rapidly during strenuous riding or walking. Always ensure that plenty of fluids are taken in, particularly in the southernmost sections of the trail, where shade cover is less and temperatures are generally higher.

It is always wise to assume that water taken from streams and rivers is unsafe to drink, particularly if there are cattle, sheep or goats in the vicinity. If in any doubt, add a water-purifying tablet to unboiled water, allowing at least 10 minutes for the chemicals to react before drinking. Water labelled *'non potable'* is not suitable for drinking.

Water source in Saint-Michel (Stage 14)

Choice of Bike
For riding the GTMC, a mountain bike is essential – a hybrid off-road/on-road bike will not be robust enough for the variety of terrain encountered on this journey. Obviously the better quality the bike, the better – aiming for a light but strong frame, with suspension if possible – but if you only have a cheap bike, don't be deterred from attempting the route, provided the bike is in good condition and well maintained. Cyclists keeping to a road route across the Massif Central are best served by a good-quality touring bicycle.

It goes without saying that which-ever you choose, it must be in a safe-to-ride condition, with an adequate braking system and a good range of working gears, particularly at the low end of the range. A good-quality cycling helmet should be worn at all times when mountain biking or road cycling (head injuries are all too com-mon and often very serious in cycling accidents). Always replace an old helmet after a few years of use, and immediately after any accident.

Spares to carry should include a tyre repair kit, including tyre levers, a set of spanners/Allen keys/screwdrivers that fit your machine (a compact multi-tool is a good idea), chain and spoke tool, two spare inner tubes, two spare sets of brake pads and a spare brake/gear cable. A good-quality cycle lock, a bicycle pump and lubricant are also essential. You will need to make a deci-sion on whether to take bicycle lights. If you go in summer when the days are long, there is no real need to carry lights, unless you intend riding back to your accommodation after dark from a restaurant or bar. However, it is essential to maintain high visibility to other road/trail users at all times, and particularly on public roads. Always wear bright colours, and consider using high-visibility reflective tabs and clothing.

Luggage

The next major decision relates to the method of carrying your equipment. Road cyclists will automatically choose panniers, but the mountain biker traditionally carries all his or her gear in a small backpack. This is fine for day riding, but the size and weight of the smallest backpack necessary, even when carrying the minimum of equipment, for a two- or three-week trip, is likely to be too much for com-fort and safe riding.

It may be possible to carry part of your equipment in a small backpack, and the remainder securely strapped to a back pannier rack, so you don't need pannier bags. The problem with panniers on a mountain bike is the constant jolting of the bags over rough terrain, but most people would find it very difficult to carry enough gear without the use of back panniers. (Don't even think of front panniers – why so many cycle tourists find these necessary is beyond me. I have been on month-long camping cycle tours without the need for front panniers, carrying more than enough equip-ment on back panniers plus bar bag.)

If using panniers on your moun-tain bike, then be sure to fit the strongest, best-quality back pannier rack that you can afford – and fit it very firmly and securely. Make sure that the attachment mechanism for your panniers onto the pannier rack is a secure and safe one, and that it is not likely to work loose with con-stant jolting. The author used back panniers while riding the GTMC with satisfactory results, but you must be tolerant of the constant jolting of your luggage.

A good quality bar bag is an excellent idea for items to which you need constant access. Buy one with a map case attached, as reference to the route will be more frequent for the mountain biker than for the road cyclist. Remember that you will almost certainly have to carry your bike from time to time over difficult sections of the route, so it is important to not only keep the luggage weight down to a minimum (see below), but also ensure that it is balanced correctly on the bike. Finally, the author encountered a couple on the GTMC towing a specially designed luggage rack at the back of a mountain bike: even this coped with the rough terrain!

Packing Light

Whether mountain biking, road cycling or walking, the golden rule on a trip such as this, unless supported with a back-up vehicle, is to keep the panniers/pack weight down as low as possible, consistent with safety and comfort. This is particularly the case when mountain biking a long-distance route, where your luggage will have to cope with constant jolting over rough terrain.

Packing light takes thought and time. Once you have assembled your basic gear, lay it out, weigh each item, and constantly ask yourself if you really need this or that. Keep a washing kit as small as possible, with a lightweight travel towel and only

Track outside Florac (Stage 10) (Alan Sides)

enough soap, toothpaste and shampoo to last you the trip. Take lightweight clothes wherever possible (this need not be expensive – Lidl and Aldi stores sell good-quality cycle clothing at very reasonable prices). You will not need many changes of basic clothing, as clothes can be washed each day and, in the usual weather conditions of southern France, should be dry by the morning. Cycling shorts and a lightweight top will be the general order of the day, but do make sure that you have the right gear to cope with extremes of weather. Although generally warm and often hot during the summer months, it can get very cold on the high-level plateau of the Massif Central, even in summer, particularly when a strong wind is blowing, and storms can produce a deluge of rain. Don't forget cycling gloves and a first-aid kit, and remember to leave enough space in your luggage for some food. To reiterate: think light, think safe.

Walkers should also think lightweight when packing for a traverse of the Massif Central. Size of pack will depend on whether camping gear is being carried – if you are relying on *gîte d'étape* and/or hotel accommodation, only a relatively small and light pack will be needed. (Over the years I have seen so many hikers struggling with enormous packs, invariably ending up at a post office to send unnecessary items home.) Good-quality lightweight boots are more than adequate for walking this trail.

MAPS

The sketch mapping in this guidebook indicates the route of the GTMC, and shows key features, but is not detailed enough to allow the trail to be followed with certainty. This is particularly so in areas where navigation is not straightforward, and within the Cévennes National Park, where GTMC waymarking is not allowed, so you are strongly advised to equip yourself with the relevant mapping.

France's national mapping agency, equivalent to the British Ordnance Survey, is the Institut Géographique National, or IGN. It produces maps at 1:25,000 and 1:100,000 scale, covering the whole country.

The most economical way of acquiring all the IGN mapping needed to follow the GTMC is to buy the official French guide to the trail, which includes all the IGN mapping at 1:50,000 in the form of a series of leaflets (see Appendix C, Further Reading). The route of the GTMC is highlighted on these maps (occasionally not exactly as waymarked on the ground).

The alternatives are to acquire either the IGN 1:25,000 (see below) or 1:100,000 scale sheets to cover the route. The 1:25,000 maps are excellent, but a total of 21 sheets is required to cover the whole of the route from Clermont-Ferrand to Sète (see below). The 1:100,000 maps, although ideal for the road cyclist, are not always detailed enough for mountain bikers following the GTMC.

1:25,000 Maps

Walkers will need IGN 1:25,000 maps. These excellent *cartes de randonnée* give detailed topographical information, including long-distance and local routes, as well as useful information for tourists. The following sheets cover the entire route, in order, from Clermont-Ferrand to Sète.

2531ET (Chaîne des Puys), 2432ET (Massif du Sancy), 2534OT (Monts du Cézallier), 2535O (Murat), 2535E (St-Flour), 2635O (Lavoûte-Chilhac), 2636O (Le Malzieu-Ville), 2636E (Saugues), 2637E (St-Amans), 2737O (Grandrieu), 2738O (Le Bleymard), 2739OT (Mont Lozère), 2640OT (Gorges du Tarn), 2641ET (Mont Aigoual), 2641OT (Millau), 2641O (Nant), 2642O (Le Caylar), 2642ET (St-Guilheim-le-Désert, 2643E (Clermont – l'Hérault), 2743ET (Montpellier), 2645ET (Sète).

The E and O at the end of each sheet number stand for *est* (east) and *ouest* (west) respectively. Areas that are particularly popular are mapped by special tourist sheets, with wider coverage than the standard sheets, and offering good value for money. These are called Top 25 maps, and are identified by a T after the map sheet code. Sheets without a T in their code are in the Série Bleue (Blue Series). The latest editions of both the Top 25 and Série Bleue 1:25,000 maps have special gridlines that allow your position on the map to be located using a GPS device.

1:100,000 Maps

At the time of preparing this guidebook (2009), the IGN 1:100,000 series is in the process of being radically updated, and when finally issued will be re-numbered, easier to read, carry more tourist and long-distance trail information than the previous series, and be GPS-compatible. This new Top 100 series of 76 sheets will cover the whole of France, compared with the 74 sheets of the old series.

IGN 1:100,000 (to be phased out by 2010/11, but some libraries will no doubt carry them for some time) sheet numbers 49, 50, 58, 59 and 65 cover the whole of the GTMC from Clermont-Ferrand to Sète.

IGN Top 100 series (to be fully introduced by 2011/12) sheet numbers 155, 162, 163 and 170 cover much of the route, but the maps for the Clermont-Ferrand region had not been issued when this guide was published.

Other Maps

Road cyclists can either use 1:100,000 IGN maps, or some of the road maps in either the Michelin Local or Region series. The following maps are required to cover the entire route.

- Michelin Local Series 1:150,000 and 1:175,000: 326 (Allier, Puy-de-Dôme), 330 (Cantal, Lozère), 339 (Gard, Hérault);
- Michelin Region Series 1:200,000: 522 (Limousin), 526 (Languedoc-Roussillon).

Free city maps, available from tourist offices in Clermont-Ferrand

and Montpellier, are useful for negotiating your way out of these cities, after which they can be discarded.

Both IGN and Michelin maps can be ordered from several British outlets (see Appendix D, Useful Contacts), or bought from numerous bookshops and newsagents locally in France. Always ensure that you are buying the latest edition.

Road Numbering

A word of caution: the road-numbering system in France is undergoing long-term reorganisation, and several road numbers will eventually change, which may include some of those in this guidebook, but vigilance, common sense and using the latest editions of maps should avoid any uncertainty. Readers can help by writing to or e-mailing the publishers if they spot any road numbers that need to be amended in the next edition (see page 4 for details).

WAYMARKING

The majority of the GTMC has standard waymarks. These consist of a square waymark with a *white* background on which is a *red equilateral triangle* next to two *red circles*. Alongside these symbols are the letters GT, followed by 'Grande Traversée du Massif Central'. The majority of these waymarks are either 12 x 12cm or 10 x 10cm in size, but some are smaller. Other mountain biking or cycling trails have the same 'triangle and two circles' waymark

symbol, but these are in a variety of colours (for example black, yellow, brown) other than red, and do not include the words 'Grande Traversée du Massif Central'. These waymarks often carry the letters VTT ('Vélo Tout Terrain') and FFC ('Fédération Française de Cyclisme'), and are found on fences, walls, posts, telegraph poles, trees and so on.

Waymarking of the route is generally of a high standard – usually quite frequent and well placed – so you should have few problems with navigation. But do bear in mind that, over time, signs can be damaged, moved, hidden, stolen, or lost for a variety of reasons (tree-felling is just one), so always be alert. Waymarking, of course, can never be perfect, and no doubt there will be times when you are having difficulty finding the route, and there will be no helpful waymarks to assist you, whereas it always seems

Waymarking on the GTMC (Stage 1)

that when the trail is obvious, there is an abundance of waymarks!

There is no GTMC waymarking for the first few kilometres of the route – from the centre of Clermont-Ferrand to Durtol on its outskirts. Thereafter the standard waymarking system is used all the way until a little after La Couvertoirade on Stage 14, with the exception of the central zone of the *Cévennes National Park*, where GTMC waymarking is prohibited. The GTMC enters and leaves the park on several occasions during Stages 9 to 13 (this is shown clearly on the maps in this book), when special care must be taken with route-finding. However, following the route description in this book, together with careful map and compass work, should result in a straightforward passage though these areas. Remember too that waymarking of GR, GR de Pays, horse-riding trails and PR trails (see below) does continue in the park, which helps greatly in the absence of GTMC waymarks.

Soon after *La Couvertoirade* the GTMC waymarking described above ends, but is replaced by waymarking for the GT34 – the Grande Traversée de l'Hérault – with which the GTMC is coincident until Saint-Jean-de-Fos, at the end of Stage 15. This waymarking is quite different from that described above. Each waymark now consists of a short green post bearing a GT34 and Hérault region stickers.

From *Saint-Jean-de-Fos to La Paillaide*, on the outskirts of Montpellier, Stage 16, the GTMC is

Waymark post for GTMC and GT34 (Stage 14)

coincident with the GR653, which bears the standard red and white waymarking of a GR trail. Some sections of this trail are very difficult for a mountain bike, so if you decide to avoid them, don't follow the red and white flashes in these areas, but follow the road bike alternative route instead.

From *La Paillaide*, near the end of Stage 16, through Montpellier and on to the Mediterranean coast at Sète, the end of the Stage 17, the GTMC carries no waymarking. However, this is not a problem, as a free city map, available from tourist offices, will allow easy navigation through Montpellier, and after that the route-finding along the Canal du Rhône is very straightforward.

It is important to be able to recognise the various other waymarking systems that are used to indicate routes in the French countryside.

The standard waymarking used by the FFRP (Fédération Française de la Randonnée Pédestre – see Appendix D, Useful Contacts) for long-distance GR trails consists of red and white paint flashes, with various arrangements of red and white lines signifying different instructions. Two sets of red/white marks appearing together indicate that a change of direction is imminent – this is often in the form of curved red and white markings pointing towards the new direction to be taken.

A painted cross, usually of one red and one white line, signals that the route is *not* in that direction – go back to pick up the correct trail. Remember also that *all* GR trails are waymarked with red and white flashes. In areas where two GR routes meet, or where a variant leaves the main route, care should be taken to follow the correct GR Trail. The GR65, which is encountered at Le Sauvage (Stage 7), is the trail to Santiago in Spain, and carries a stylised pilgrim's shell as well as the usual red/white waymarks.

Occasionally you will see other waymarks: GR de Pays are red and yellow, whereas PR trails are usually single yellow, or sometimes green or blue stripes. Orange waymarks are for horse-riding trails – they sometimes occur in the shape of a hoof-print.

Certain notices should also be understood. *'Propriété privée'* or *'Défense d'entrer'* means that the area is private and entry forbidden. The signs *'Réserve du chasse'* and *'Chasse privée'* do not refer to mountain bikers or walkers, but mean that hunting rights are reserved for the owner of the land.

Signposts showing the distance in kilometres to the next place on the route will also be encountered from time to time, These usually carry self-explanatory symbols indicating the location of a *gîte d'étape*, campsite, café or restaurant.

From time to time the route of a trail may change. This can be for a variety of reasons – to improve the route, to avoid problems such as a land slip or an eroded path, or sometimes at the request of a landowner. As time goes on, there may be changes to the line of the GTMC such that the route described in this guidebook is not always the one on the ground – if this is the case, always follow the waymarks rather than trying to find the route described here, until the original route is re-joined.

TRAINING

Those who cycle (whether on a mountain bike or road bike) regularly, or walk in the hills of Britain, should have no difficulty on the GTMC. However, if you haven't taken any exercise for some time, a programme of training in the months preceding the trip would be sensible – an unfit person would find the ride or walk a great strain, and miss out on much of the enjoyment of the experience. Remember too that the three activities covered in this guidebook – mountain biking, road cycling and long-distance walking – use different muscles and require different skills, so be sure that you are well prepared for whichever method you choose to travel the GTMC.

Cyclists who have done little off-road mountain biking would be well advised to practise as much as possible on off-road routes, starting a minimum of six months before setting off on the GTMC. Begin with short rides, then full day rides, and finally a weekend or preferably week of off-road cycling. Get as much training as you can on moderately difficult terrain, where there are tree roots, muddy ruts and rough stones on the surface, and where some of the ascents/descents

are steep. However, do not worry if your previous mountain biking experience is mainly confined to relatively easy off-road tracks. Take things easy, and never attempt a section on your bike of which you are unsure. In most cases, the length of the stages is such that there is time to complete the route in a day even if a fair percentage is walked.

The safest and most sensible option when faced with a difficult and/or potentially dangerous section is always to dismount and push the bike, and even this may not be that easy, so be sure to get plenty of practice pushing and riding a heavily laden bike over steep ground.

It is hard work pushing uphill (Stage 11)

HEALTH

Perhaps the most common ailment that befalls travellers abroad is stomach upset or diarrhoea. Rest and light meals often provide the best cure, although a non-prescription medicine will help to ease the symptoms. Failure to correct stomach upsets can lead to weakness, dehydration and further complications.

Colds and other minor ailments are usually easily treatable with medication from a pharmacist (small supermarkets, grocers and newsagents in France do not usually stock medicines such as paracetamol, aspirin and cold relief powders), but it is advisable to include basic medications in a first-aid kit.

Over-exposure to the sun and heat stroke are other problems to be avoided at all costs. Always wear a helmet when cycling, but otherwise a sun hat, and sunglasses and high-factor sunscreen. If the weather becomes very hot, then set off early in the morning and have a long siesta during the heat of the day. Drink plenty of liquid to prevent dehydration, and cover exposed skin that is unused to a southern sun.

Mountain bikers should pay particular attention to the contents of their first-aid kit, ensuring that they have enough dressings and antiseptic to cope with the cuts and bad grazing that might result from a fall. Some means of strapping a limb until assistance is found is a good idea, and if you are travelling in a group, at least one member of the group should consider going on a first-aid course before the holiday.

SNAKES

The European viper, or adder, is not uncommon in the Massif Central, and a bite, although unlikely to be fatal, would be exceedingly unpleasant. It could also have serious consequences in more sparsely populated regions, where help may not be quickly available. Vipers are less of a threat to the biker than to the walker (except of course when the former is pushing his or her bike, which no doubt will happen from time to time on the GTMC).

Fortunately, snakes are fairly secretive animals, likely to detect a walker's presence by vibrations along the ground and take avoiding action, but do keep a good lookout for them, in order to avoid accidentally treading on one. It is a good idea to be familiar with the markings of the European viper (dark green/black in colour with characteristic zigzag stripes on the upper surface), although the chances are that the GTMC will be completed without ever catching sight of even one.

A bite from a viper can result in considerable bruising, discolouration and swelling of the surrounding area, and in the unlikely event that you are bitten, be sure to rest, avoid a panic reaction, and get medical help as soon as possible.

EMERGENCIES

The emergency services (medical help, police or fire brigade) can be reached by dialling 112. This service is staffed by French speakers, and they are unlikely to speak much English, but there is an 'SOS Help' service in English, which can be contacted by dialling 01.47.32.80.80, or from a UK mobile, 00.33.1.47.32.80.80 (it would be sensible to programme this into your mobile before you set off).

LANGUAGE

The French, like the British, are not particularly keen on learning foreign languages. Many younger people can speak some English, but in general do not expect the level of fluency found in Holland, Germany or Scandinavia. This is particularly true of the rural areas of the Massif Central. It is a good idea to brush up 'rusty' French before the holiday, as even the most elementary grasp of the language will pay dividends by enriching your experience in France. However, no true adventurer will be discouraged by an inability to speak the local tongue, even if it necessitates the occasional use of sign language!

MONEY/BANKS/TELEPHONE

The unit of currency in France is the euro. Credit and debit cards are accepted widely, and are a useful form of payment for hotel bills, restaurant meals and rail tickets.

There are banks in Clermont-Ferrand, Allanche, Saint Flour, Bagnols-les-Bains, Le Pont-de-Montvert, Florac, Sainte-Énimie, Montpellier, Sète and Nîmes, as well as a few smaller branches in some of the other towns and larger villages en route (some of the latter may be only open one or a few days per week, and then only for a few hours). It is advisable to carry plenty of currency from the outset.

Mobile phone coverage is variable, depending on the service provider and topography, and is fairly unreliable in many of the more remote areas of the route, although virtually every village has a public phone box. However, it is now extremely rare to find a public telephone in France that accepts coins, so if you intend to make use of public phones it is a good idea to buy a French Telecom phonecard, easily available from most newsagents and general shops, on arrival in France.

INSURANCE

It is advisable to take out travel and medical insurance, as rescue and hospitalisation charges can be very expensive. Ensure that the policy covers you for the activities you plan to undertake – mountain biking, cycling or walking. Make sure too that an adequate medical sum is insured and, except for cyclists keeping to the national road system, that the costs of mountain rescue are included. The

A tricky stream crossing (Stage 3)

latter should include the use of a helicopter to lift an injured biker/walker off the hills.

Certain rights are available for British subjects in France under reciprocal National Health Service arrangements within the EU, so it is a good idea to have a European Health Insurance Card, which is free (for an EHIC application form and further information, either enquire at post offices in Britain, go to www.dh.gov. uk/travellers or telephone 0845 606 2030).

PUBLIC HOLIDAYS AND TIME

There are more public holidays in France than in Britain, although between June and October there are only two to consider – Bastille Day on 14 July and the Fête of the Assumption on 15 August.

On both of these days the public transport system is affected and shops may be closed, although most cafés and restaurants stay open. In the spring there are public holidays on 1 May (May Day), 8 May (1945 Armistice Day) and on Whit Monday. In the autumn, bank holidays fall on 1 November (All Saints Day) and 11 November (1918 Armistice Day).

French time is one hour ahead of the time in Britain, so French summer time is one hour ahead of BST and French winter time one hour ahead of GMT.

USING THIS GUIDEBOOK

Layout

The GTMC is divided into 17 stages, each of a length that the average mountain biker should be able to complete in a day, although information is included to allow more than one stage, or less than a complete stage, to be ridden in a day, depending on the fitness, experience and aspirations of the biker. Each stage ends where some form of permanent overnight accommodation is available, usually a choice of hotels, *gîtes d'étape* or *chambres d'hôtes*. The walker will take more than one day for most of these stages, but again enough information is included to allow you to make accommodation arrangements.

Road cyclists will often ride two or even more of these stages in a day.

Each stage begins with a summary table showing the total distance and ascent/descent for the stage, the distances between intermediate points, in both miles and kilometres, and an estimate of the percentage of the route that is off-road. Heights above sea level are given for the beginning and end of each stage, and for cols and some of the villages en route. This allows the basic details of the day's itinerary at be seen at a glance. Towns and large villages where there is a choice of accommodation, shops, cafés and restaurants are shown in upper case in the table, and the start and finish points of each stage are in bold. The figures in square brackets

Welcome to Orcival (Stage 1)

– [x/y] – at stage finish points are the kilometres ridden from Clermont-Ferrand followed by the kilometres remaining to Sète.

After the summary table a short précis of the stage is given, followed by a section entitled *Facilities*, which summarises the opportunities for refreshments and accommodation of all types along the way and at the end of the stage. Note that where 'shop' is mentioned, this refers principally to grocery shops, supermarkets, bakers and the like, where food may be purchased. The information under *Facilities* will allow those who wish to shorten or lengthen the day's ride/walk to find somewhere to spend the night. Details of other facilities, such as banks, post and tourist offices, are also included here. Although these sections of the guide give an indication of the facilities likely to be found, the listings cannot be comprehensive, and it is recommended that you acquire an up-to-date list of accommodation and other facilities along the GTMC before leaving for France, or on first arrival in the area, from local tourist offices (see Appendix D, Useful Contacts).

The section *Places of Interest* includes the main points of interest on or near the trail, summarised here so that the day can be planned effectively. To make the most of your visit to the region, which has a rich history and culture, as well as outstanding landscape features, *Places of Interest* should be used in conjunction with a tourist guidebook.

Next comes *GTMC Mountain Bike Trail* – the mountain bike route description, which should be read in conjunction with the map in this guidebook and the relevant IGN map. Special attention has been paid to areas where route-finding may be a problem, or where waymarking is particularly poor. Where alternative routes are possible, details of these are given, and if there are more difficult and potentially dangerous sections ahead, these are mentioned, and ways to avoid them suggested. Remember that what is extreme for some will be considered fairly easy, run-of-the-mill mountain biking for others, and always exercise great caution, as well as respecting other trail users, particularly walkers.

The next section, *Road Bike Alternative*, describes one, or often two, suggested road routes between each of the major locations on the GTMC, suitable for touring cyclists. For the most part these make use of minor roads, which carry relatively light traffic, although the quantity and type of traffic does vary with the season, becoming heavier during July and August. It also depends on the hour of the day, with huge milk tankers on some of these rural roads early in the mornings, for example. These routes can also be followed by mountain bikers who either want a day away from riding the trails, or to avoid a difficult section of the trail, or to revert to the road network if there is a lot of rain, which will make the tracks very

Making good progress towards Pierre-Plantée (Stage 8) (Alan Sides)

muddy. The maps for the road bike route are all together in a separate section – Stage Maps for the Road Bike Alternative – after the end of Stage 17 and before the appendices.

Finally, *Walking Trail* addresses the person following the GTMC who for the most part would use the route described for the mountain biker. Advice on avoiding longer sections of road walking is given, and the various alternative GR trails are outlined. Those who opt for some of the latter, not included on the GTMC, will need the relevant Cicerone or French Topo guides. (See Appendix C, Further Reading, for full details.) Also included in this section is information on how the stages may be split to allow comfortable distances to be walked each day, and how to find accommodation for the night.

42

Distances and Altitudes

Distances are given only in metres and kilometres in the route description, as IGN maps are metric (distances in miles as well as kilometres are in any case given in all of the summary tables). For anyone unfamiliar with metric units of distance, a metre is just a little over a yard, and to convert kilometres to miles divide by 1.6 (approximately). Main summits and cols are given in both metres and feet, but the majority of other heights in metres only. A very approximate conversion is 1000m equals about 3300ft. When the word 'metres' appears in the text, this refers to linear distance, whereas 'm' after a number denotes altitude in metres.

STAGE 1

Clermont-Ferrand to Laschamp

Distance	56.0km (34.8 miles)	Ascent	934m (3064ft)
Off-road	71%	Descent	490m (1607ft)

Location	Distance (km)		Distance (miles)	
	Sectional	Cumulative	Sectional	Cumulative
CLERMONT-FERRAND (380m)				
Durtol	3.8	3.8	2.4	2.4
Blanzat (507m)	6.2	10.0	3.8	6.2
Malauzat	3.2	13.2	2.0	8.2
VOLVIC (490m)	3.7	16.9	2.3	10.5
Volvic water factory	0.9	17.8	0.6	11.1
Le Viallard	2.7	20.5	1.7	12.8
Les Brossons (788m)	2.9	23.4	1.8	14.6
Grelière	4.7	28.1	2.9	17.5
Lambertèche	1.3	29.4	0.8	18.3
Le Vauriat (875m)	5.6	35.0	3.4	21.7
Beauregard	2.9	37.9	1.8	23.5
Southeast of Puy de Côme (1026m)	9.8	47.7	6.1	29.6
Col de Ceyssat (1078m)	4.9	52.6	3.1	32.7
LASCHAMP (967m) [56/662]	3.4	**56.0**	2.1	**34.8**

Once you set out from Clermont-Ferrand you are beginning the long journey to the Mediterranean, although this at first appears not to be the case, as the route almost immediately heads north to the small town of Volvic, famous throughout the world for its pure spring water.

Don't be in a rush to exit Clermont-Ferrand, as this large industrial city has a charming centre, with a splendid cathedral at its heart. Then be sure to allow some time to visit the water-bottling factory just outside Volvic, before heading off across country, first westwards to Le Vauriat, and then finally south to pass through fascinating wooded countryside dotted with long-extinct volcanoes. The Puy de Dôme is the highest in the region, and the most celebrated, with a steep tarmacked road winding its way to the very summit, but the bike (VTT) route sticks to tracks and paths through the woods – trails that are often muddy, with many protruding tree roots and rocks, so beware! The *gîte d'étape* in Laschamp is a pleasant place to spend the night (and perhaps lick your wounds after the first stage on the trail).

Cyclists may like to take a day and a half over this stage, particularly if they have perhaps travelled up from Nîmes on the morning train. After a few hours sightseeing and lunching in Clermont-Ferrand, Volvic can easily be reached in a

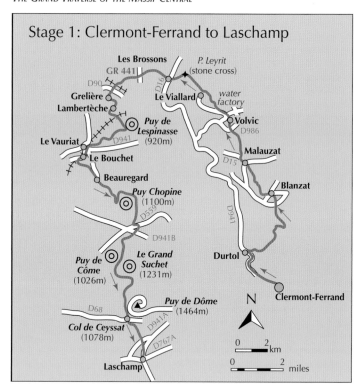

Stage 1: Clermont-Ferrand to Laschamp

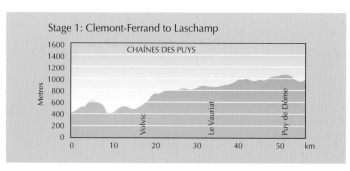

Stage 1: Clemont-Ferrand to Laschamp

few hours on the first day. This will also allow more time to look around Volvic and its water factory on the second day, before continuing on the ride to Laschamp. This tactic is also a sensible one, so as not to overdo things on the first day.

Facilities

Clermont-Ferrand, the capital of the *département* of Puy de Dôme, and by far the largest city in the whole region, has an abundance of the facilities expected of such a metropolis. A large *maison du tourisme* is situated in Cathedral Square – l'Espace Massif Central, Place de la Victoire. There are hotels of all categories, as well as a youth hostel and an Éthic Étape for budget accommodation. Restaurants of all grades and café–bars abound, with *épiceries* large and small, department stores and supermarkets. There are several cycle shops, so if you need any equipment or spares, now is the time to buy.

Malauzat, south of Volvic, has a hotel–restaurant, Les Moulin des Gardelles. The Hôtel-Restaurant du Commerce in the centre of Volvic can be recommended for both accommodation and food. Volvic has several shops, including *épiceries* and a *boulangerie*, and a choice of restaurants and cafés. For further information, consult the *office du tourisme* in the centre of town. Tiny Le Vauriat offers a café en route, near the railway line, and there are inns at the Col de Ceyssat. There is a *gîte d'étape* about 5km east of this col, off-route in the village of Ceyssat.

Rose window, cathedral, Clermont-Ferrand

Those climbing the Puy de Dôme will find a large and expensive hotel-restaurant, Le Dôme, at the very summit, where there is also a café.

This stage ends in Laschamp, where there is a *gîte d'étape*, as well as a *gîte d'étape*/hotel–restaurant complex (Espace Volcan).

Places of Interest
Clermont-Ferrand
The home of Michelin tyres. The attractive city centre radiates from the large and open l'Espace Massif Central, on which stands a massive 13th-century Gothic cathedral.

Volvic
Famed for its dark volcanic stone (andesite) and the world-famous mineral water that bears the town's name. A visit to the free Volvic Water Visitor Centre is a must, with its excellent audio-visual presentations (English soundtrack available). See also the town's Romanesque church of Saint-Priest and, if there is time, the pictur-esque Château de Tournoël, situated 1.5km to the north.

Puy de Dôme and the Volcans d'Auvergne
At 1464m (4800ft), the Puy de Dôme is the highest peak in the Monts-Dôme region of the Auvergne. A road leads to the very top – for those with the energy!

GTMC MOUNTAIN BIKE TRAIL

If arriving at the central railway station in Clermont-Ferrand, make your way to the l'Espace Massif Central, Place de la Victoire, the official starting point of the GTMC, on the south side of the cathedral. Head south on Rue Terrasse to Place Sugny, soon reaching the Place de Jaude (equestrian statue). Ride ahead here along Rue Blatin to reach Rue Gabriel-Péri. At a T-junction turn left on Rue Fontgiève (D941A). Continue ahead on Avenue Raymond Bergougnan, uphill to turn right at a crossroads on the Rue du Limousin, signposted to Volvic, heading towards Durtol.

Immediately in front of Durtol Cemetery turn *sharply* to the right to find the first GTMC sign of the route. Follow the signs uphill. A viewpoint is reached, from where there is an excellent view of Clermont-Ferrand below, with the Puy de Dôme visible to the south. On reaching a telecommunication tower turn left, leaving the surfaced road to sample your first section of off-road cycling. Follow the waymarked trail across the plateau, until the descent (care, particularly in wet conditions) to the left towards Blanzat.

Approaching Blanzat

In the centre of Blanzat cross the road and ride ahead at the 'WC Publics'. Leaving Blanzat the road becomes a gravel track. Remain on this until you reach a track junction, where you turn left on the Balade de Vignerons. At Malauzat follow the D15 in the direction of Volvic. At the end of the village take a tarmacked track to the right, which you follow to the outskirts of Volvic. Cross the main D986 road (care) to head into the centre of Volvic.

The GTMC mainly follows the route of the GR441 from Volvic to Le Vauriat. Leave Volvic on the minor road to the right of the *office de tourisme*, signposted to La Vierge. Climb on this to reach a point from where a short detour may be taken to visit the Volvic Water Visitor Centre (highly recommended).

Up until this point the biking route has been generally easy, but from now on, all the way to Laschamp, the tracks and paths are often more difficult to negotiate, particularly after rain, when sections of the trail are often very muddy and sometimes waterlogged. Tree roots along the trail demand respect!

The waymarked trail climbs to the hamlet of Le Viallard and from there heads northwest, until a left turn at the P. Leyrit stone cross takes you to the southern end of the small community of Les Brossons. Cross the D16. Waymarks take you first to the northwest, but after about a kilometre swing towards the west-southwest, crossing first a minor road to the south of Beaunit and later a railway line and the D90, to follow a minor road into the hamlet of Grelière.

Central square in Volvic

Tracks head southeast and then southwest to a second hamlet – Lambertèche. Soon after this settlement turn left to cross a railway line and continue into woodland. After about 1.5km be sure to take a waymarked right turn, south of the Puy de Lespinasse. After a further 0.6km, at a junction, turn left to follow the trail towards Le Vauriat (café), the latter stages of which may be very muddy. Take care on the short section on the D941 on the final approach to Le Vauriat.

Turn left, leaving the D941 to follow the railway line towards Le Bouchet. Skirt to the east of this hamlet, then turn left to head southeast. At the cross, a little before Beauregard, turn left to enter the hamlet. Continue southeastwards for about 2km, where there is a sharp left turn on a main track heading north. After about 0.5km turn right to skirt Puy Chopine, firstly in an east-southeasterly direction, gradually bending to head south and then south-southwest, to reach the D559.

Turn left along the D559 for about 250 metres, then right to cut across to the main D941B, which can be busy. Left along this road for 100 metres, before turning right to head along a track into the woods. After about 1.2km take a left fork, now heading southwards to pass between the Puy de Côme, on the west, and Le Grand Suchet, on the east, two prominent volcanic puys.

At the southern end of the Grand Suchet, be sure to head eastwards for about a kilometre, before continuing in a southerly direction to pass to the west of the Puy de Dôme. Progress along this section can be slow, with mud, tree roots, steep sections and eroded paths to contend with.

The road (D68) at the Col de Ceyssat (café – refreshment) is reached after about 2.5km. Turn left to pass the inns and then right along a path. Take care on the steep, eroded, and possibly muddy section here. This trail leads all the way to the D941A, a distance of approximately 1.8km. Cross this main road (care) and continue ahead for another 800 metres to reach the outskirts of Laschamp at the D767A. Turn right to enter the village.

ROAD BIKE ALTERNATIVE

See 'Stage Maps for the Road Bike Alternative', after the end of Stage 17.
Follow the GTMC to Durtol (see above for a detailed route description) and then minor roads to Nohanet and Sayat. From there take the D15 or D15A north to Volvic. Leave the town on the main D941, direction Pontgibaud, but leave it after a few kilometres to head south on minor roads (D407, D776, D90) to Chanat-la-Mouteyre and Temant.

Continue on the D90 south, crossing the D941B, to reach the main D941A. Head southwest along this for about 3–4km to take the turn-off on the left, the D767A, to Laschamp. Before doing so, very fit cyclists may wish to test their hill-climbing abilities on the mountain road up to the summit of the Puy de Dôme. It is 40km from Clermont-Ferrand to Laschamp (omitting the detour up the Puy de Dôme).

WALKING TRAIL – 2 DAYS

There is about 5km road walking from the centre of Clermont-Ferrand to just beyond the suburb of Durtol, so non-purists may wish to take a bus to Durtol to start the walk from there. Nevertheless, the walking out through the centre of Clermont-Ferrand is full of interest. Thereafter, all the way to Laschamp, only about another 5km is on tarmac, in small sections along the way.

Volvic is easily reached in a day's walking from the centre of Clermont-Ferrand, but only the very fittest long-distance walkers will manage the 39km from there along the GTMC to Laschamp in a day. There is very little opportunity for acquiring accommodation between Volvic and Laschamp, but the walker is served by a considerably shorter, more direct route of 27km between these two villages. Follow the GR441 from Volvic southwest over the Puy de la Nugère to join the GR4, which is coming in from Le Vauriat to the northwest, at the Puy Chopine. From there follow the GR4/GR441/GTMC southwards, over, if time and stamina allow, the summit of the Puy de Dôme, all the way to Laschamp. This is a fine route, with excellent views, and the opportunity for refreshment en route in the café/restaurant on the top of the Puy de Dôme.

STAGE 2
Laschamp to Murol

Distance	47.0km (29.2 miles)	Ascent	660m (2165ft)
Off-Road	74%	Descent	760m (2493ft)

Location	Distance (km)		Distance (miles)	
	Sectional	Cumulative	Sectional	Cumulative
LASCHAMP (967M)				
Recoleine (932m)	6.8	6.8	4.2	4.2
Neuville	4.4	11.2	2.8	7.0
Voissieux	1.8	13.0	1.1	8.1
Juégheat	1.0	14.0	0.6	8.7
ORCIVAL (850m)	3.1	17.1	1.9	10.6
Pessade (1100m)	10.5	27.6	6.5	17.1
Mareuge (1060m)	5.4	33.0	3.4	20.5
Saignes (1058m)	3.9	36.9	2.4	22.9
BEAUNE-LE-FROID (1030M)	3.2	40.1	2.0	24.9
Varennes (960m)	1.8	41.9	1.1	26.0
Lac Chambon (875m)	1.2	43.1	0.8	26.8
MUROL (800m) [103/615]	3.9	**47.0**	2.4	**29.2**

The trail heads southwestwards on leaving Laschamp. This second stage takes the rider or walker from the northernmost of the great Massif Central ranges, the Monts Dôme, to their southerly neighbour, the Monts-Dore, the high mountains centred around the town of Le Mont-Dore, a little to the west of the area covered by the GTMC.

The route undulates, sometimes offering easy riding, sometimes on more difficult tracks, but the views over the Chaîne des Puys and towards the distant Puy de

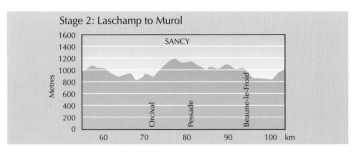

Stage 2: Laschamp to Murol

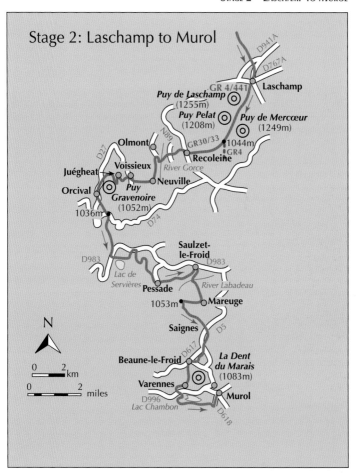

Stage 2: Laschamp to Murol

Sancy make the effort worthwhile. Orcival, with its ancient church and relaxing cafés, offers a welcome break before the trail changes direction to head southeast-wards through a mixture of open country and woodland, passing through several quiet villages and hamlets, eventually dropping quite steeply down to picturesque Lac Chambon and the large village of Murol, where an overnight can be spent at a hotel or campsite.

Facilities

Between Laschamp and Recoleine, about 1.5km off-route to the south, is the Château de Montlosier, where there is a *gîte d'étape*, as well as a headquarters and information centre for the Parc Naturel Régional des Volcans d'Auvergne.

Orcival, a large tourist village, has shops, cafés, restaurants, hotels, a *gîte d'étape* (at the Lac de Servières, 4km from the village) and a tourist information office. Saint-Bonnet-près-Orcival, 3km north of Orcival, has *chambres d'hôtes* and a campsite. Another *gîte d'étape* will be found in the small village of Pessade, which also has a restaurant, Le Balladou.

There is a *chambres d'hôtes* in the village of Beaune-le-Froid, while near the shore of Lac Chambon will be found both a café–restaurant and a campsite. The large village of Murol, to the east of the lake, and the end of today's stage, has shops, *chambres d'hôtes* and hotels (the Hôtel de Paris is recommended – bikes are stored safely undercover overnight).

Places of Interest
Chaîne des Puys

Chaîne des Puys is the term for the complex chain of volcanic plugs, or *puys*, that formed during various geological periods, but which are now all long extinct. Those with the time available will be well rewarded by further exploration of the many other hills that make up the chain.

Typical puy scenery

Orcival

Don't leave without a visit to the renowned 12th-century church in the centre of the town.

Parc Naturel Régional des Volcans d'Auvergne

Opened in 1977, this park, the largest of the French regional nature parks, includes the Monts Dôme, Dore and Cantal, and the high plateaux of the Cézallier and Artense.

Murol

Murol dates from the 13th century, as does the ruined château that overlooks the village. Visitors are attracted by nearby picturesque Lac Chambon, which is popular with anglers.

GTMC MOUNTAIN BIKE TRAIL

Leave Laschamp on the GR4/441 heading south-southeast, signposted to Pessade. The trail passes to the east of the Puy de Laschamp and Puy Pelat, and to the west of the Puy de Mercœur, to arrive, about 4km after Laschamp, at a track junction, at map spot height 1044m. Here the trail to Pessade, the GR4, turns to the southeast, whereas the GTMC now follows the GR30/33 southeast and then east to Recoleine.

Pass under the N89 to follow a track that crosses a minor lane in just over a kilometre. After crossing the River Gorce the route swings to the northwest, heading towards Olmont, but before entering this hamlet, take the track that heads south to Neuville. On reaching the outskirts of the village turn right, now heading west, to reach a second village, that of Voissieux.

At Voissieux a sign indicates the way to Juégheat – cross the D27 and follow the track to this village. Here climb to the south to a viewpoint to the east of the Puy Gravenoire, and then head north for a while, before the route bends to the left to join the D27, which you follow to the south to enter Orcival.

After a visit to Orcival, follow GTMC waymarks to return to the D27, turn left and shortly right to leave this road, and begin a steep climb to the south, out of the of the valley, eventually reaching the D74. Turn left along this, but only for about 100 metres, to map spot height 1036m. Here turn right off the road.

After a kilometre turn left to head through woodland to reach the D983. Turn right on this road for about 600 metres, before turning left off it, to head west towards the Lac de Servières. Pass along the northern shore of the lake, to follow the main track heading downhill to re-emerge at the D983. Turn right along this road for about 250 metres, before leaving it on the left to head south back into the wood. Follow the waymarked route from here to Pessade.

Entering Orcival

After Pessade there is a section of easy cycling for a while on well-surfaced tracks, with several 90° well waymarked turns, on a trail that generally heads east-northeast towards Saulzet-le-Froid. At a crossroads to the south of the village, turn right, within 600 metres crossing the Labadeau stream, and continue in a south-easterly and then southerly direction to the hamlet of Mareuge. From here follow the tarmacked *route forestière*, heading initially to the west.

After 1.5km, near map spot height 1053m, turn left at a junction, and after another 600 metres leave this road to head in a southeasterly direction to descend to the village of Saignes, located on the west side off the D5. Cross this road to head south, after 1.5km rejoining the D5 near its junction with the D617, which is followed into picturesque Beaune-le-Froid.

From the village head south, to the west of La Dent du Marais. Descend quite steeply. On reaching Varennes follow the GTMC signs across the D996. The way continues to the Lac Chambon, following its southern shore to reach a café and campsite, after which you soon reach the main road, the D618, and follow it northwards to the centre of Murol.

ROAD BIKE ALTERNATIVE

See 'Stage Maps for the Road Bike Alternative', after the end of Stage 17.
The busy but scenic D941A leads, in a little over 5km, to the N89. Cross over this main highway to take the D216, which heads southwards, becoming the D27 before reaching Orcival in just under 8km. Remain on the D27 for a further

couple of kilometres, before turning left on the D74, following this scenic road to Vernines. Continue along the D74 heading south to the D983, then remain on the D74, now heading eastwards, to Saulzet-le-Froid. The D74 continues to the east to reach the scenic D5, which is followed south to Murol. 41km from Laschamp to Murol.

For a more direct route to Murol, omitting a visit to Orcival, head southeast from Laschamp on the D52 to Beaune, and from there take the D778 to Fontfreyde. Negotiate a short section of the main N89 before escaping south on the scenic D90, crossing the D213 and passing the Lac d'Aydat. The equally scenic D5 leads south all the way to Murol. 29km from Laschamp to Murol.

WALKING TRAIL – 2 TO 3 DAYS

The GTMC principally follows the GR4 and then the GR30/33 to Orcival and from there the GR441 to Pessade – both good walking routes. Strong walkers could make Pessade in a day, but those wanting a more leisurely journey could easily break at Orcival, where there is accommodation.

The alternative is to follow the GR4 directly from Laschamp to Pessade, a distance of 20.3km. The latter route is described in Cicerone Guide *Walks in Volcano Country* (see Appendix C).

The GTMC section from Pessade to Murol is in good walking country, on paths and tracks, with only short sections of minor road walking, the latter totalling only about 15 per cent of the total 19.4km.

Village fountain in Beaune-le-Froid

STAGE 3
Murol to La Godivelle

Distance	34.0km (21.1 miles)	Ascent	821m (2693ft)
Off-road	73%	Descent	336m (1102ft)

Location	Distance (km)		Distance (miles)	
	Sectional	Cumulative	Sectional	Cumulative
MUROL (800m)				
Bessolles	4.0	4.0	2.5	2.5
Saint-Victor-la-Rivière (1018m)	0.8	4.8	0.5	3.0
Serre Haut	3.5	8.3	2.2	5.2
BESSE-EN-CHANDESSE (1000m)	2.6	10.9	1.6	6.8
Lac Estivadoux	4.0	14.9	2.5	9.3
Creux de Soucy	2.1	17.0	1.3	10.6
Lac de Montcineyre (11809m)	2.8	19.8	1.7	12.3
Chaumiane	2.7	22.5	1.7	14.0
Escouailloux (1050m)	1.5	24.0	0.9	14.9
Cureyre (1180m)	1.2	25.2	0.7	15.6
Brion-Haut (1270m)	4.0	29.2	2.5	18.1
LA GODIVELLE (1220m) [137/581]	4.8	**34.0**	3.0	**21.1**

This stage, although relatively short, offers some rough riding, so don't expect to make rapid progress. The day starts with a climb out of Murol to Saint-Victor-la-Rivière, from where there are good views back to the Dents du Marais, above and to the north of Lac Chambon. The trail heads south and negotiates a river crossing before reaching popular Besse-en-Chandesse. This town, often bustling with tourists in season, is also known as Besse et Saint-Anastaise, or by locals as simply Besse.

More climbing as the GTMC continues via Lac Pavin to the Lac de Montcineyre, an idyllic spot for lunch. The section that follows can be very muddy after wet weather, before the trail becomes easier, although there is another fairly steep climb from the farm hamlet of Escouailloux to that of Cureyre. Then at last an easy section follows, on good tracks across a high plateau, with extensive views of the Sancy range – identify the Puy de Sancy itself, at 1886m (6186ft) the highest peak not only in the Auvergne, but in the entire Massif Central.

More cross-country rough stuff from Brion-Haut to La Godivelle, but those who are thinking 'I will never go mountain biking again!' have the option of a much easier road alternative.

The *gîte d'étape* at La Godivelle has good food and hospitality and is situated in a delightful rural upland setting, on the Cézallier plateau, between two small

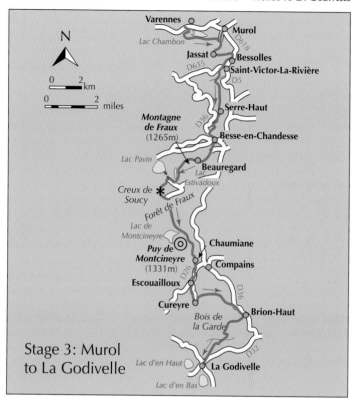

Stage 3: Murol
to La Godivelle

picturesque tarns. This is a good place to totally relax, away from the cares of the world, and prepare for the rides to come in the days that follow.

Facilities

A *gîte d'étape* is located off-route, in the hamlet of Courbanges, 3km west of Saint-Victor-la-Rivière, but the most concentrated facilities on today's route will be found in the small touristy town of Besse-en-Chandesse, which has an abundance of shops, restaurants, cafés and hotels, as well as a campsite.

Between Besse and La Godivelle there are two *gîtes d'étape*, at Chaumiane, and at day's end, La Godivelle (the latter is recommended for its food and hospitality). Note that there is no shop in La Godivelle, so buy supplies at Besse.

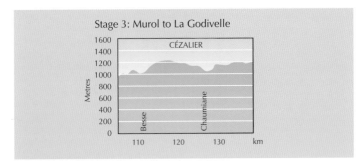

Stage 3: Murol to La Godivelle

Places of Interest
Besse-en-Chandesse
A small town which, because of its range of medieval and renaissance buildings, is very popular with tourists.

Puy De Sancy and the Monts-Dore
The Puy de Sancy, at 1886m (6186ft), is the highest mountain of the Monts-Dore range, which towers above the large town of Le Mont-Dore, to the west of our route. The mountains are, alas, rather disfigured by the pistes and paraphernalia

Primitive crucifix

of this popular skiing area, centred on the ski resorts of Le Mont-Dore and Super-Besse, the latter just a few kilometres from Besse-en-Chandesse on the GTMC.

La Godivelle and its two Lakes

A tranquil spot to spend the evening, exploring the two picturesque tarns situated on either side of the village, one above and one below.

GTMC MOUNTAIN BIKE TRAIL

The day begins with a climb up to Saint-Victor-La Rivière. Return to the D618, climbing south out of Murol, soon bearing right on the minor road that leads to the lake, but after only 200 metres bear left to rejoin the waymarked GTMC trail. Turn left after a further 300 metres to cross a second lane and continue to the outskirts of Jassat, from where you climb eastwards to the D5, near the hamlet of Bessolles.

The GTMC keeps to the west of the D5, ascending to the top of the hill, where there is a large ornamental crucifix at Saint-Victor-La Rivière (an easier option is simply to stay on the D5 for just over a kilometre to reach Saint-Victor). There are good views of the surrounding mountains from here.

Head southwest on the D635 for 200 metres to take a left turn heading south, soon descending steeply to cross a river, which may be quite tricky to cross (beware in times of flood). Climb south from this river to reach the hamlet of Serre-Haut. The trail continues in a southerly direction, partly on the D36, to descend to the small tourist town of Besse-en-Chandesse.

The GTMC climbs out of Besse towards the south to meet, after 600 metres, a minor road. Ride south on this, direction Chandèze, but leave it on the right after 200 metres to climb to the viewpoint of Beauregard. Continue over the Montagne de Fraux, to the west and later southwest, to pass Lac Estivadoux and rejoin the minor road. Turn right on this road for 500 metres to a T-junction at map spot height 1261m.

Turn left here for the GTMC, but for a visit to large, circular, picturesque Lac Pavin (recommended, particularly for its viewpoint) keep ahead here for 600 metres, but return to this point to resume the trail. The forest road heads south-southwest, and 300 metres after passing the Creux de Soucy, when the road bends to the left, continue ahead on a track to the edge of the Forêt de Fraux. Here turn right to head south, crossing a stream at one point, to reach the northeastern shore of the Lac de Montcineyre, a good spot for a rest and a bite to eat.

Head east on a track away from the lake for 350 metres, bearing to the right at a junction to skirt below the tree-covered *puy* of Montcineyre. After about 700 metres the often muddy route through the forest heads southwards to the hamlet

Time for a snack by Lac de Montcineyre (Alan Sides)

of Chaumiane, to the west of the village of Compains, which can be clearly seen from here. From Chaumiane a minor road is taken south to the D26, which is then followed to Escouailloux. A steep climb follows, on a minor road, to the farm hamlet of Cureyre.

Leave Cureyre to follow good tracks heading eastwards and later southeastwards across the plateau of the Montagne de Barbe Sèche and the Montagne de Blatte, to eventually join the D36. Turn right along this road to enter Brion-Haut. Those wanting a quick and easy ride to La Godivelle should remain on the D36 to its junction with the D32, turning right on this for about 5km to reach the village. However, the GTMC leaves Brion-Haut on a track heading southwest.

After a little over a kilometre, turn left to head for the forest, the Bois de la Garde. Turn left to skirt the edge of this wood for about 300 metres, then take a path that enters the trees. The trail follows the GR30. There should be a bridge to cross the next river, after which the GTMC continues in a southwesterly direction to reach the D32. Turn right along this road to reach La Godivelle within 800 metres.

ROAD BIKE ALTERNATIVE

See 'Stage Maps for the Road Bike Alternative', after the end of Stage 17.
Scenic roads abound in this area. From Murol head south on the D5 to Besse-en-Chandesse, and from there take the D36 past the Lac de Bourdouze to Compains.

Remain on this road to Brion, and on southeastwards to its junction with the D32. Follow this southwestwards to La Godivelle. 34km from Murol to La Godivelle.

Other pleasant routes between Besse and Compains are possible, including the D633 via Le Fayet and the D619 via La Veissière, with then either the D127 and D26 or the D127 and D624 to Compains.

WALKING TRAIL – 1 TO 2 DAYS

Very strong walkers could cover this stage in a day. For those choosing to take two days, the best place to stay the night would be Besse-en-Chandesse, a pleasant and interesting small town with accommodation, although this does split the route into two very unequal halves.

The GTMC follows considerable sections of the GR30, which also weaves its way from Murol to La Godivelle, to the west of the GTMC, during the first half of the route to Lac Pavin, southwest of Besse, and later detouring to visit Compains before reaching Brion-Haut. An alternative would be to follow this GR trail all the way to La Godivelle, but if splitting the stage, a detour to Besse would probably have to be made to find accommodation.

Cycling in the afternoon sun (Alan Sides)

STAGE 4
La Godivelle to Allanche

Distance	30.5km (18.9 miles)	**Ascent**	283m (928ft)
Off-road	33%	**Descent**	558m (1830ft)

Location	Distance (km)		Distance (miles)	
	Sectional	Cumulative	Sectional	Cumulative
LA GODIVELLE (1220m)				
Jassy	8.5	8.5	5.3	5.3
Boutaresse (1212m)	2.3	10.8	1.4	6.7
Col de Chamaroux (1291m)	3.6	14.4	2.2	8.9
Buron de Paillassère-Bas	3.6	18.0	2.2	11.1
Col de Fortunier (1280m)	4.9	22.9	3.1	14.2
Pradiers (1170m)	2.1	25.0	1.3	15.5
Le Bac	4.1	29.1	2.5	18.0
ALLANCHE (960m) [167.5/550.5]	1.4	**30.5**	0.9	**18.9**

Only the most committed mountain bikers would want to follow the official GTMC trail from La Godivelle to the small village of Jassy. The route recommended here takes to minor roads to the north and east of La Godivelle, a most pleasant section that also provides excellent views of the surrounding hills.

Today's stage is easier for bikers than the previous one, much of it on quiet minor roads or good firm tracks. It is on road south from Jassy to the village of Boutaresse, from where another road is climbed to the Col de Chamaroux, beneath the summit of 1475m (4838ft) Mont Chamaroux.

The road is left behind here, for a good track that climbs high above Boutaresse, offering excellent views of the surrounding hills and plateaux of the

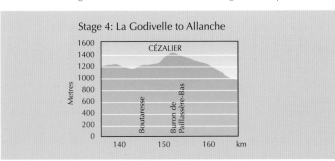

Stage 4: La Godivelle to Allanche

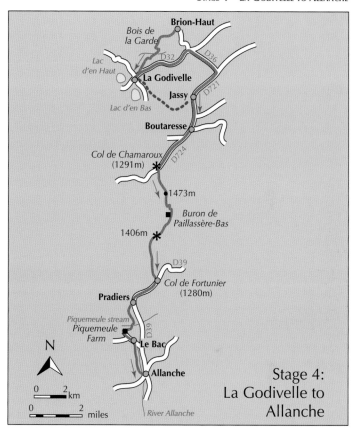

Stage 4:
La Godivelle to
Allanche

Monts-Dore, Cézallier, Forez, Mézenc and the Monts de Cantal. A high point of 1473m is reached before the trail continues south to the Col de Fortunier, then there is more road into the village of Pradiers. A little 'rough stuff' riding follows, with a descent to the valley and then into the small town of Allanche.

Strong mountain bikers could combine this relatively short stage with the next one, which also contains a considerable amount of road cycling, thereby making a long but relatively easy day of 72.5km. Both Stage 4 and Stage 5 involve considerably more descent than ascent, as the trail descends from the high Auvergne plateau to the wide valley separating it from the Margeride.

Facilities

Once you have left La Godivelle, no facilities of any description will be found today until you reach the end of the stage at Allanche. But in this small town there are plentiful shops, cafés and restaurants, as well as a hotel, Le Relais des Remparts, and a nearby campsite, at Pont Valat, 1.5km south on the GTMC, heading for Maillargues (see Stage 5)

Places of Interest
Cézallier Plateau

A high, extensive volcanic tableland situated between the Monts-Dore and Cantal mountains.

Allanche

The reasonably sized settlement of Allanche still retains some of its ancient ramparts. The 11th-century church is worth a short visit. The wide River Allanche rises in the hills of the Cézallier plateau, to the north of the eponymous town.

GTMC MOUNTAIN BIKE TRAIL

The official route of the GTMC climbs over a high stile (!) at the northeastern edge of La Godivelle, then follows a very rough route, poorly defined on the ground, heading southeastwards. It passes immediately to the north of the Lac d'en Bas, and later to the north of the Lac de Saint-Alyre, before reaching a narrow tarmacked lane that heads northeast into Jassy. Experienced mountain bikers may wish to take this route, but it does entail lifting bikes and luggage over the stile, and this difficult route is certainly not recommended in bad weather conditions, as it is high and exposed.

The recommended route, described here, is all along pleasant minor roads to Jassy. Leave La Godivelle heading northeast on the D32. After 4.5km, turn right at the junction with the D36. Follow this road for about 2.5km, then take a right turn on the D721 that leads into Jassy.

From Jassy remain on the D721 to Boutaresse, where you take the D724 in the direction of Marcenat. Climb on this quiet road, heading southwest for about 4km to the Col de Chamaroux (1291m). Here take the wide track to the left, climbing to a viewpoint at a map spot height of 1473m. This good track continues to the Buron de Paillassère-Bas, and then on to another excellent viewpoint at 1406m. After a further 3km the track joins the D39 at the Col de Fortunier (1280m). Turn right on the D36 to follow this road for about 2km into the charming village of Pradiers.

On the old track to Buron de Paillassère-Bas

The quickest and easiest ride into Allanche is south along the D39 all the way into the town, a distance of about 4.5km. But the GTMC takes a more difficult cross-country route to the west of the road. At the southern end of the village, near the cemetery, turn right along a track, which eventually descends very steeply on stony ground, where care is required, to cross the Piquemeule stream and emerge on a minor road at Piquemeule Farm. Turn left along this lane to reach the D679, which is followed to the left. At Le Bac leave this road by turning off to the right through the hamlet. After 100 metres turn left to follow the course of the River Allanche southwards, eventually bearing left to reach the centre of the town.

ROAD BIKE ALTERNATIVE

See 'Stage Maps for the Road Bike Alternative', after the end of Stage 17.
Two road routes around the Cézallier mountains are possible, one to the east and one to the west. The eastern route at first follows the mountain bike route on minor roads to Boutaresse, described above, but then takes the D721 via Parrot and Le Luguet to Anzat-le-Luguet. Here change direction, on a hilly route south-westwards on the D23 via Apcher and Vins-Haut to the junction with the D39, and maintain direction on this to Pradiers. From this village head south along the D39, which joins the D679 just before Allanche. 42km from La Godivelle to Allanche.

Enjoying a break in Pradiers

The western route takes the D32B southwest out of La Godivelle, and later the D636 to Montgreleix and on to join the D36 in the Boujon valley. Follow the D36 westwards to its junction with the D104. Climb southwestwards on this road to meet the D679 at Marcenat. Follow the D679 southeastwards all the way to Allanche. 34km from La Godivelle to Allanche.

It is, of course, possible to combine these two routes, by taking the former to Boutaresse, from where you follow the D724 southwestwards until it joins the D36...and so continuing with the second option above, via the D104 and Marcenat.

WALKING TRAIL – 1 DAY

Again, this stage is achievable by strong walkers in a day. From La Godivelle take the true line of the GTMC to Jassy, a cross-country route of about 4km. Cross the stile at the northeastern edge of La Godivelle and follow the GTMC waymarks heading southeast, passing to the north of both the Lac d'en Bas and then the Lac de Saint-Alyre. Bear to the left (northeast) at a point to the northeast of the peak of Le Testou (1327m) to reach the southern outskirts of the hamlet of Jassy.

By following this true line of the GTMC, rather than the road route recommended for GTMC bikers above, some 8.5km of road walking is avoided, and the total walking distance for the day is reduced to a more manageable 26km. From

Leaving La Godivelle

then on to Allanche, about half of the route is along roads, but these are all minor lanes, with very little traffic, and make for fast and easy walking, the whole adding up to a very pleasant walking trail.

Before setting out on the route, the walker needs to make a major decision at La Godivelle. The alternative to the GTMC route from here to Saint-Flour is to first follow the GR30 west from La Godivelle to Espinchal and on to Egliseneuve-d'Entraigues in the Rhue valley, a distance of some 10km. In this small town the GR4 is rejoined and can be followed all the way to Saint-Flour via Condat, Lugarde, the Cantal volcanos, Valuéjols and Le Saillant. This splendid walk of 106km takes in most of the main peaks of the Cantal region, including Puy Mary and the Plomb du Cantal. The trail is described in the Cicerone Guide *Walks in Volcano Country* (see Appendix C), and will take the average walker five days to complete.

STAGE 5
Allanche to Saint-Flour

Distance	42.0km (26.1 miles)	**Ascent**	496m (1627ft)
Off-road	52%	**Descent**	636m (2086ft)

Location	Distance (km)		Distance (miles)	
	Sectional	Cumulative	Sectional	Cumulative
ALLANCHE (960m)				
Maillargues (1000m)	1.9	1.9	1.2	1.2
Nuis (1062m)	4.8	6.7	3.0	4.2
Mouret (1056m)	0.6	7.3	0.3	4.5
Chalinargues (1058m)	5.5	12.8	3.4	7.9
NEUSSARGUES (799m)	9.1	21.9	5.7	13.6
Savignac (910m)	6.9	28.8	4.3	17.9
Le Saillant	5.2	34.0	3.2	21.1
Andelat (860m)	2.2	36.2	1.4	22.5
Roueyre (800m)	2.4	38.6	1.5	24.0
SAINT-FLOUR (770m) [209.5/508.5]	3.4	**42.0**	2.1	**26.1**

The mixture of minor roads and forest tracks on this stage generally means easy biking, and good time should be made. The section after Neussargues in particular is perhaps one of the easiest so far. Nevertheless, there are cross-country sections where especial care is required.

The GTMC generally heads in a southerly direction, but weaving from side to side as it visits a number of villages, the most interesting and picturesque being that of Chalinargues, with its large impressive church bell tower, characteristic of this region of rural southern France. A grand panorama opens out of the Alagnon valley before the trail descends a steep gorge to the town of Neussargues, although

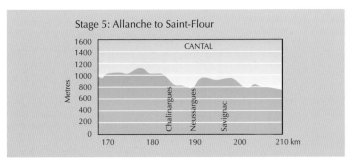

Stage 5: Allanche to Saint-Flour

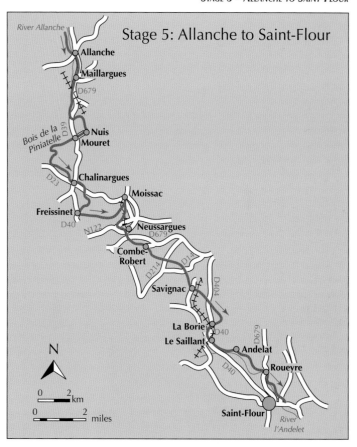

Stage 5: Allanche to Saint-Flour

the very short detour into Moissac, on the way, will be rewarded with the sight of another splendid bell tower, at the top of the village church.

The riding for the most part is relatively easy from here on, mainly on good quiet narrow country lanes. The formidable Château of Le Saillant is passed on a descent to the village of Andelat, from where further descent leads to Roueyre, a village now little more than a suburb of Saint-Flour. The actual route of the GTMC skirts Saint-Flour's old *ville-haute* ('high town'), but you may wish to detour for a visit, or better still, stay overnight in this historic part of the town, rather than bypassing it to reach the lower, more modern part of Saint-Flour.

If you are looking for a day off from the trail, Saint-Flour is a good choice, as it has much to interest and delight the visitor, with many pleasant cafés in which to relax, and fine restaurants where lost calories can very easily be replaced.

Facilities

A basic *gîte d'étape* is located in the village of Chalinargues, but more facilities are to be found at much larger Neussargues, where there are cafés, restaurants, shops, including a supermarket, a hotel – the Hôtel des Voyageurs – a campsite and a railway station.

The second half of the day has few facilities other than a café at Andelat, but Saint-Flour has everything that one might expect of such a large town and tourist centre. This includes up to a dozen hotels, *chambres d'hôtes*, many restaurants and cafés, a tourist office (situated in the main square, Place d'Armes, in the upper town), shops of all kinds, including supermarkets, several banks and a post office. Saint-Flour is on the main Clermont-Ferrand to Béziers railway line, and the train station is in the lower town.

Where the GTMC descends to the lower town it emerges onto a main road, just before a large open square, and at this point the Hôtel-Restaurant Le Pont Vieux is conveniently situated on the left (note, however, that this is not the best

Bells of Chalinargues church

location from which to explore the much older and more interesting *ville-haute*). The *camping municipal* site is at Avenue Docteur Mallet, on the south edge of town, near the River Ander, and there is another campsite to the north of the town (follow the N9).

There is often a large market in the square in Saint-Flour lower town, where the GTMC emerges at the end of this stage. This is a good place to buy fruit or cheese, and stock up generally before the continuing journey south.

Places of Interest
Chalinargues and Moissac
The medieval churches in both of these villages have large, traditional external bell towers, each bearing four large bells.

Le Saillant Castle
This château is most impressive, built high on a huge natural rock, but alas is not open to the public.

Saint-Flour
The medieval fortified town of Saint-Flour, the judicial and spiritual centre of the High Auvergne, is situated on the edge of a promontory of basalt rock, with the modern extension to the town below. The 15th-century cathedral in the heart of the *ville-haute* is an austere Gothic building, famous for its statue of Christ, carved from dark wood, the only 'black Christ' in France. The town houses several museums, the most notable of which is the Musée de la Haute-Auvergne, located next to the cathedral. Several houses dating from the 15th and 16th centuries will be found in the town, particularly fine examples of which are in Rue Marchande and Rue de Thuile.

Cantal Volcanoes
The Cantal region of the Massif Central is to the west of Saint-Flour. It contains many of the highest mountains in the Auvergne, all of them long extinct volcanoes. The most notable peaks are the Puy Mary (1787m, 5861ft), the 'Matterhorn of the Cantal', and the Plomb du Cantal (1855m, 6084ft).

GTMC MOUNTAIN BIKE TRAIL
Leave Allanche heading south on the D679, after about 1.7km turning left onto the minor road that enters Maillargues (or alternatively stay on the D679 for a further 600 metres until its junction with the D39). Follow waymarks to reach the D679/D39 junction. Take the latter road until, after crossing a railway line, turn

Looking towards Moissac

right on a track and left again within 150 metres. Head south to rejoin the D39 after about 1.6km.

Go straight ahead on this road, but leave it after only 100 metres by taking the first turn on the left (if you remain on this road you will reach Mouret within just over a kilometre, without visiting Nuis). Follow this minor road through the Bois de Nuis to reach the hamlet of the same name, then continure to follow the minor road southwest to the village of Mouret.

Cross the D39 and follow the track to the Moulin du Pic (remaining on the D39 heading south will lead directly to Chalinargues in about 3km). Follow waymarks, generally in a southwesterly direction, through the Bois de la Piniatelle to meet the D23. Turn left almost immediately on a track that heads southeastwards to reach Chalinargues, in about 2.5km.

Leave this village heading southeast on the D23, and after about a kilometre take the first track on the right. After a further 800 metres take the track to the right, which leads to the hamlet of Freissinet. (Note that the D40 south from Chalinargues leads directly to Freissinet in about 1.8km.) Those wishing to avoid the difficult section after Freissinet should remain on the D23 via Moissac and down to Neussargues.

Leave Freissinet heading east on the trail that soon offers extensive views of the Alagnon valley and Neussargues below. A very steep and difficult section follows: take special care here. The trail then crosses a railway line and reaches the D23, south of Moissac. Turn right on this road, but soon leave it by taking the first track on the right. Head south, soon following the railway line to reach and cross the Route National 122 opposite Neussargues.

After a visit to Neussargues follow the D679 in the direction of Saint-Flour. After the tunnel, head right towards Celles on the D34, but soon leave it by taking the first road on the left to Combe-Robert. Pass a communal oven in Combe-Robert, then take a narrow lane that climbs to a cross. Turn left here and continue, crossing both the D214 and the D14 to arrive in the village of Savignac.

Cross a railway line and bear to the right, heading southeast on a surfaced track, crossing the D404 and continuing for another 1.5km to reach a cross-tracks. Turn right to pass the farm of La Borie, then soon reach the D40. Cross the railway line to descend past the château of Le Saillant, continuing on the D40 towards Andelat.

The quickest and easiest route to Saint-Flour from here is to remain on the D40 all the way into the town. However, the GTMC climbs the minor road to Andelat. From this village the trail heads east-southeast, and then south, to descend to Roueyre. Cross the D679, climbing on a narrow lane, then taking a track to the right after about 200 metres. Continue ahead on this to pass the Moulin de Massalès, eventually descending to a junction of roads in the lower town of Saint-Flour.

Le Saillant

ROAD BIKE ALTERNATIVE

See 'Stage Maps for the Road Bike Alternative', after the end of Stage 17.

Leave Allanche heading south on the D679 to Neussargues, a ride of some 13km. Alternatively, for a quieter route to Neussargues, leave the D679 at Maillargues for the D39, via Mouret to Chalinargues. From here take the D23 via Moissac to Neussargues. Cross the main N122 at Neussargues, to continue along the D679 all the way to Saint-Flour.

Alternatively, a more rural route takes the D34 from Neussargues to Celles, from where the D40 leads via Secourieux, Coltines, Vaux and Le Saillant to Saint-Flour – this is a very scenic and relatively easy route. 36km from Allanche to Saint-Flour (on the direct D679 route).

A good alternative would be to leave the D679, 1.5km south of Allanche, at Maillargues, to climb steeply eastwards either on the D309 or the D114 to Peyrusse. From this village pick up the D14 heading southeast to the N122 and then southwards, still on the D14, via Valjouze to meet the D679 at Talizat. Left along this road leads to Saint-Flour in 12km . 42km from Allanche to Saint-Flour.

WALKING TRAIL – 2 DAYS

Stage 5 divides neatly into two day-walks, each of approximately the same moderate length (21.9km on the first day and 20.1km on the second day), with an overnight at Neussargues, where there is hotel and camping accommodation.

The walk is not overtaxing, with only moderate ascent and descent on each of the two days. Over half of the trail is off-road, while the rest is along peaceful country lanes.

STAGE 6
Saint-Flour to Paulhac-en-Margeride

Distance	43.0km (26.7 miles)	**Ascent**	1002m (3287ft)
Off-road	69%	**Descent**	638m (2093ft)

Location	Distance (km)		Distance (miles)	
	Sectional	Cumulative	Sectional	Cumulative
SAINT-FLOUR (770m)				
Saint-Georges	3.9	3.9	2.4	2.4
Le Pirou (890m)	3.8	7.7	2.4	4.8
RUYNES-EN-MARGERIDE (900m)	6.6	14.3	4.1	8.9
Forêt Domaniale de Pinols	12.1	26.4	7.5	16.4
Croix de la Donne (1357m)	2.3	28.7	1.4	17.8
Musée de la Résistance (1330m)	5.2	33.9	3.3	21.1
Summit of Mont Mouchet (1497m)	4.1	38.0	2.5	23.6
Auzenc (1280m)	2.7	40.7	1.7	25.3
PAULHAC-EN-MARGERIDE (1180m) [252.5/465.5]	2.3	**43.0**	1.4	**26.7**

We now leave the High Auvergne behind to head for a second area of high plateaux and wooded hills – the remote and sparsely populated Margeride. This area
is so remote and off the beaten track that it was a favourite hiding place of the
French Resistance during the Second World War, and many undercover operations
began here. Sadly, therefore, it was also the scene of several atrocities between
the resisting French and the Nazi forces. The national memorial to the *maquis*, or
French Resistance fighters, now stands high on these hills at Mont Mouchet, and
a visit to this and the adjacent museum is highly recommended, no detour being
necessary, as our trail passes right by.

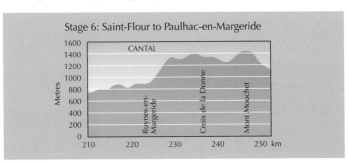

Stage 6: Saint-Flour to Paulhac-en-Margeride

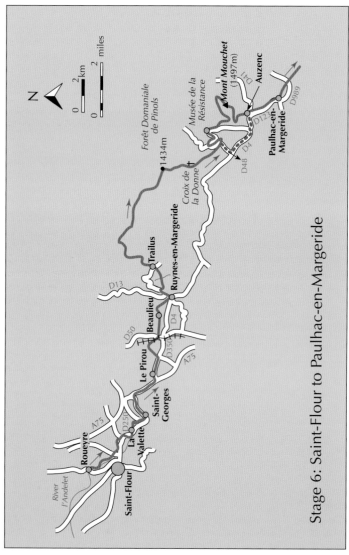

Stage 6: Saint-Flour to Paulhac-en-Margeride

But before reaching Mont Mouchet there is much uphill work to be done, although the first section of the day to the village of Ruynes-en-Margeride, one of the largest in the Margeride, is a relatively easy ride. Enjoy the facilities in Ruynes, before the long and often steep ride (push!) up to the ridge that lies some 450m (1500ft) above and to the east of the village. Easy and enjoyable riding follows on good, wide, generally firm forest tracks, until the road system is encountered once more, for the ride up to the National Resistance Monument.

After a visit to the museum and café, there is the opportunity to climb to the summit of 1490m (4887ft) Mont Mouchet itself. Many will no doubt be pushing their bikes on the final stages, but the climb is certainly worth the effort, both for the satisfaction of doing so, and particularly for the splendid view from this memorable vantage point – the whole of the Margeride laid out before you, with distant hills visible on the horizon. Enjoy the long descent into tranquil Paulhac-en-Margeride, for an evening in *gîte d'étape* or *auberge*.

Facilities
Saint-Georges has a hotel, Le Bout du Monde, and so too has Ruynes-en-Margeride, Hotel Moderne. The large village of Ruynes also has a *chambres d'hôtes*, shops (including a *patisserie* with gorgeous cakes) and a café, as well as a municipal campsite, Le Petit Bois. No facilities will be found, of course, in the hills of the Margeride, but a welcoming café–restaurant, the Auberge du Mont Mouchet, is located near the Museum of the Resistance. Charming but small Paulhac-en-Margeride has a *gîte d'étape*, an *auberge*–restaurant, Le Bon Accueil, but no shop.

Places of Interest
Garabit Viaduct
One of France's most impressive Belle Époque railway viaduct spans the wide Truyère valley about 5km to the southwest of Ruynes-en-Margeride (worth a detour if there is time).

The Margeride
A huge and remote area of the Massif Central, between the Velay to the east, the Cantal to the west, the Cézallier to the north and the Cévennes to the south. Much of the land is depopulated high plateau, often windswept and very cold in winter.

The National Monument to the French Resistance and the Museum of the Resistance
Situated below the summit of Mont Mouchet, the Monument National à la Résistance et aux Maquis de France stands in a forest clearing alongside the Musée de la Résistance. A visit here, although a sobering experience, is a highlight of the day.

Stone memorial to the Resistance, Mont Mouchet

Mont Mouchet

Mont Mouchet, at 1497m (4910ft), is the highest peak in the Margeride, a fine viewpoint, well worth the effort to reach. The *table d'orientation* on the summit identifies all the main features in the surrounding landscape.

GTMC MOUNTAIN BIKE TRAIL

Leave Saint-Flour, initially following signs to the A75 motorway, later taking the road heading southeast towards Saint-Georges. Near the hamlet of La Valette, climb on the left, following waymarks to reach the D250. Turn right to enter the village of Saint-Georges. Follow the lane that heads northeast towards the A75. The lane then turns to follow alongside the A75, eventually reaching a junction where you turn left to cross a bridge over the motorway and enter Le Pirou.

Leave the village on the D4, heading eastwards. After 1.3km leave the road by turning left at the road junction with the D350, which goes to the right at this point. (Those wanting the easiest and quickest ride to Ruynes-en-Margeride should remain on the D4 all the way to this village). After a kilometre, at a cross-tracks, turn right to ride towards the south to meet the D4 again. Take this road under the railway, almost immediately turning left on the D50, direction Vabre. In about 100 metres turn right on a track heading east. About 500 metres after passing the hamlet of Beaulieu, turn right at a roadside cross and head southeast to the village of Ruynes-en-Margeride.

Enjoy a rest in the café here, before setting out on a major hill climb into the mountains of the Margeride. Ride out of Ruynes heading north on the D13. After about 600 metres turn right, signposted to Trailus. Almost immediately turn right off this minor road to take a track that crosses a stream, before climbing steeply into the hills to reach the mountain hamlet of Trailus (an easier alternative would be to remain on the lane to Trailus).

At the exit of the hamlet leave the road to take a track on the left, continuing the steep ascent. The waymarked trail enters the forest and makes a number of turns before eventually emerging onto a major ridge, where you turn to the right, soon reaching a fine viewpoint. You have just completed a climb of around 450m (about 1500ft) and justly deserve a good rest here.

The wide excellent forest track heads sout-eastwards along the forested ridge for about 3.5km to reach a track junction. Fork right here on another track for a further 2.5km to reach the edge of the Forêt Domaniale de Pinols, at a map spot height of 1434m. Turn right here to descend towards the south to reach, in about 2.3km, a metal cross (the Croix de la Donne). From the cross continue on the wide forest track for another 2.5km to reach the D48.

At this point a decision must be made. The shortest and easiest ride to Paulhac is by turning right on the D48, which meets the D4 in about a kilometre. Turn left on this road for about 2km to a road junction, where the road to Mont Mouchet turns left. Ignore this, but continue on the D123 via Auzenc towards Paulhac-en-Margeride.

A much more rewarding, but longer and harder route, allowing a visit to the museum and monument to the French Resistance at Mont Mouchet, turns left on the D48. After about a kilometre turn right on the signposted road to the Resistance museum. After a visit here, there are again two options. The shortest and easiest route is to remain on the road heading south until it meets the D123. Turn left on this to ride via Auzenc to Paulhac.

The much harder, mountain biking route leaves the forest road about 700 metres after the museum by taking a track to the left. After a kilometre turn sharply to the left on another track heading northeast. After about 1.6km turn very sharply to the right, now climbing to the southwest to reach the toposcope on the summit of Mont Mouchet (1497m). Continue the traverse over the mountain, heading south-southwest at first, eventually dropping steeply down to Auzenc. The minor lane descends, crosses the D41, and arrives in just over 2km at the village of Paulhac-en-Margeride.

ROAD BIKE ALTERNATIVE

See 'Stage Maps for the Road Bike Alternative', after the end of Stage 17.

Leave Saint-Flour, initially on the mountain bike route described above, but keep to minor roads to cross over the A75 *autoroute* to Le Pirou. Follow the D4 eastwards from here to Ruynes-en-Margeride. From this large village the D4 continues generally east-southeastwards, passing through Clavières to a road junction for Mont Mouchet. From here the D123 and finally the D989 are followed to Paulhac-en-Margeride. 35km from Saint-Flour to Paulhac-en-Margeride.

However a better, albeit quite hilly route, would be to leave the D4 7km after Clavières on the D48 heading north. This meets the D41 in 6km. Turn right along this road to complete a circuit of Mont Mouchet to arrive eventually in Auzenc. Turn south on the D123 and finally the D989 to reach Paulhac in about 2.5km. 49km from Saint-Flour to Paulhac-en-Margeride.

Those wanting to visit the museum and monument to the French Resistance should leave the D48 less than 2km after it departs from the D4, to follow the road signposted to the museum, reached in just over a kilometre.

Heading towards Paulhac-en-Margeride

Houses in Auzenc

WALKING TRAIL – 2 DAYS

Again, this stage of the GTMC divides conveniently into two day-walks. The first, from Saint-Flour to Ruynes-en-Margeride, is a short, relatively easy half-day walk of 14.3km, but this is fortunate, as it leaves a full morning to explore the interesting, historic town of Saint-Flour before leaving. There is accommodation of most types in the attractive village of Ruynes-en-Margeride.

The second day over the Margeride is quite demanding, 28.7km, and with substantial ascent and descent. However, the full length of the route can be shortened considerably (by 4km) by making a direct line to Paulhac in the latter stages, omitting a visit to Mont Mouchet and the Resistance museum and monument.

The hills and high plateaux of the Margeride offer excellent walking, and there are other options for crossing this region on foot. The major contender is the GR4, which heads southeast from Saint-Flour, and after passing through Le Pirou keeps to the south of the GTMC. It passes through Combechalde, from where a variant route heads off to Ruynes-en-Margeride, later rejoining the main trail of the GR4 near La Chassagne, south of Ruynes.

From there the trail continues on its southeasterly bearing, passing through La Besse, Paladines, Chaulhac and Saint-Léger-du-Malzieu, to reach the larger village of Le Malzieu Ville. The GR4 then heads over the hills to the east, to l'Estival, before turning southeast again to La Roche and Sainte-Eulalie, a small village which is about 2.5km to the west of the GR43/GTMC, south of Le Sauvage (Stage 7).

STAGE 7
Paulhac-en-Margeride to Le Giraldès

Distance	52.7km (32.7 miles)	**Ascent**	825m (2706ft)
Off-road	80%	**Descent**	598m (1961ft)

Location	Distance (km)		Distance (miles)	
	Sectional	Cumulative	Sectional	Cumulative
PAULHAC-EN-MARGERIDE (1180m)				
Vachellerie (1195m)	2.4	2.4	1.5	1.5
East of Truc de la Garde (1420m)	9.7	12.1	6.0	7.5
Chanaleilles (1150m)	5.8	17.9	3.6	11.1
Le Sauvage (1270m)	6.1	24.0	3.8	14.9
La Baraque-des-Bouviers	13.2	37.2	8.2	23.1
La Croix du Bas (1480m)	0.9	38.1	0.6	23.7
Col de la Croix de Bor	2.2	40.3	1.3	25.0
Col des Trois Sœurs (1452m)	2.7	43.0	1.7	26.7
LE GIRALDÈS (1300m) [305.2/412.8]	9.7	**52.7**	6.0	**32.7**

Not the easiest of stages, both in terms of terrain and navigation, although there are several miles of relatively easy cycling with clear navigation along good tracks. A considerable length of the trail traverses woodland, but there are also many open sections with good views.

The route goes in a generally southeasterly direction to the village of Chanaleilles, which will no doubt be your first stop to enjoy coffee in a village café. The Domaine du Sauvage is an ancient farmstead that has been receiving guests for centuries, as at this point we are crossing the route of the famous pilgrim trail to Santiago de Compostela, in northwestern Spain. Here is a good

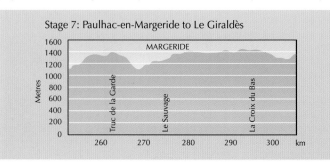

Stage 7: Paulhac-en-Margeride to Le Giraldès

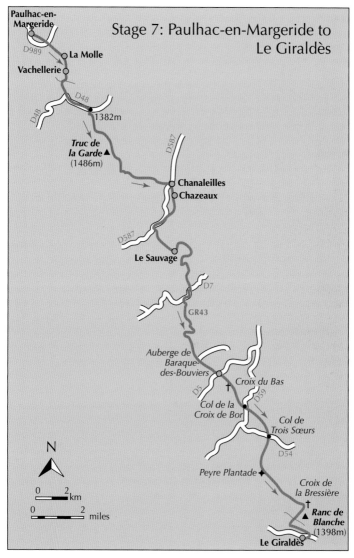

Stage 7: Paulhac-en-Margeride to
Le Giraldès

Paulhac-en-Margeride

D989

La Molle

Vachellerie

D48

D48

1382m

Truc de la Garde ▲
(1486m)

D587

Chanaleilles

Chazeaux

D587

Le Sauvage

D7

GR43

Auberge de Baraque-des-Bouviers

D5

† *Croix du Bas*

Col de la Croix de Bor

D59

Col de Trois Sœurs

D54

Peyre Plantade ✦

Croix de la Bressière †

▲ *Ranc de Blanche*
(1398m)

Le Giraldès

N

0   2 km

0   2 miles

place to enjoy a picnic lunch before pressing on through forest, where careful navigation is needed, as the trail passes to the east of the village of Sainte-Eulalie, eventually reaching the D5 at La Baraque-des-Bouviers.

After another convenient stop for refreshment in the café at the Auberge de Baraque-des-Bouviers, there is some relatively easy riding over the high, forested plateau to the south, passing ancient marker crosses and track junctions, and over two shallow cols. Nevertheless, you may encounter some muddy sections of track and some more difficult terrain, before easier riding leads down, sometimes steeply (so care is required), to the small settlement of Le Giraldès.

Facilities

Although the trail never enters any settlement of a reasonable size on this stage, there are several places where refreshment and accommodation are available. Chanaleilles, a small village built on a hillside just above a valley, has two cafés, one with a small store. Le Sauvage, on the popular Santiago pilgrim trail, is a large, ancient farmstead with a *gîte d'étape*. The Domaine du Sauvage is on a high open plateau, and a grand place to spend the night. The Auberge de Baraque-des-Bouviers is a café–restaurant with rooms and a *gîte d'étape*. This stage terminates at the small village of Le Giraldès, which although devoid of a shop, offers a cosy *gîte d'étape*, renowned for its excellent homemade cuisine and hospitality. You will probably be eating dinner with the family, a lengthy affair in a very homely atmosphere, where the courses seem to never stop coming.

GTMC and GR65 meet

Places of Interest

Le Sauvage and the Santiago Trail

The celebrated pilgrim trail from Le Puy to Santiago de Compostela in northwestern Spain, of medieval origin, has enjoyed a popular revival in recent years. The trail, around 1500km long, crosses the GTMC at the 18th-century farmstead of Domaine du Sauvage.

Sainte-Eulalie and the European Bison Reserve

The small village of Sainte-Eulalie is the gateway to the Réserve de Bisons d'Europe. Founded in 1991, the reserve, open to the public, is one of the last sanctuaries of the European bison, which once roamed the huge forests of Europe. The 40 animals here originally came from Poland.

GTMC MOUNTAIN BIKE TRAIL

From the church a minor lane leads eastwards to Diéges on the D989. Continue sout-east through La Molle to Vachellerie. Leave the lane here, eventually descending to cross a stream. Climb towards the south, reaching the D48 after about 2.5km. Turn left to follow this road for approximately 1.7km, to map spot height 1382m.

Here turn right onto a forest track. Follow this track, passing to the east of the Truc de la Garde (1486m), and continue to a junction, about 5km after leaving the road. Take the lower track here, heading generally in an easterly direction to eventually descend to reach, after about 4km, the village of Chanaleilles.

Descend from the village church, turning left on the road for about 250 metres, to take the first minor road on the right, signposted to Madrière. This passes under high-tension electricity cables to approach the settlement of Chazeaux. Take a track on the right and follow the trail as it heads south, parallel with the D587 to the west, eventually passing back under the electricity wires to rejoin the road (this route can be a little difficult to follow, but a simple alternative is to take the D587 south from Chanaleilles to this point, a distance of around 2km). Continue south along the D587 for a further kilometre to turn left on the wide, signposted track to Le Sauvage.

From the large *gîte d'étape* complex of Le Sauvage, care is needed with navigation, as the trail follows many twists and turns through the forest. Follow the waymarks carefully and you should emerge at the D7 after about 5.5km. Turn right on this road, heading southwest, leaving it to take the first waymarked track on the left. From this point onwards the GTMC follows the GR43 (Draille de la Margeride – red/white waymarks) for most of the way to Peyre Plantade, about 5.5km before Le Giraldès.

Along the track to Giraldès

Auberge de Baraque-des-Bouviers

Head south, reach and pass an extensive viewpoint, and then watch carefully for waymarks, as there are several changes of direction for the next 1.5km. The trail then maintains a southeasterly direction for about 3km through the forest to emerge at the Auberge de Baraque-des-Bouviers on the D5.

Easy cycling follows for the next 6km. Cross the road and follow the track for about a kilometre to reach the Croix du Bas. Maintain a southeasterly direction to cross the D59 at the Col de la Croix de Bor. Continue ahead on the track to cross the D54 at the Col de Trois Sœurs. From here the track heading south can be very muddy, and hence difficult to negotiate.

After about 2.4km turn left at a junction at Peyre Plantade, and then maintain a southeasterly direction for 3km. Near the Croix de la Bressière, bear right to head southwest, passing to the west of the Ranc de Blanche (1398m). After crossing a stream, take the first track on the left to ride for a further 1.5km to the southeast, beginning a steep descent (care). Finally, turn sharp right to continue the descent to Le Giraldès.

ROAD BIKE ALTERNATIVE

See 'Stage Maps for the Road Bike Alternative', after the end of Stage 17.
From Paulhac-en-Margeride, head south on the D989 to Malzieu. From here there are two routes to Saint-Alban-sur-Limagnole – either the direct D4, or the longer but more scenic D14 via Lajo to its junction with the D587, and then southwest along this road to Saint-Alban.

Continue on the D4 and later the D58 to Saint-Denis-en-Margeride, from where a minor road leads to La Villedieu. Follow the Truyère valley southwestwards along the D34, leaving it after a few kilometres to climb south on the D59 to Estables. From here follow the D3 eastwards to Le Giraldès. 57km on the D4 route to Saint-Alban, or 68km on the D14 route to Saint-Alban, from Paulhac-en-Margeride to Le Giraldès.

Those interested in an optional hill climb to reach a good viewpoint can take the minor road that leaves the D3 about halfway between Estables and Le Giraldès and which heads south to the summit of the Truc de Fortunio (1551m).

WALKING TRAIL – 2 DAYS

The GTMC between Paulhac and Le Giraldès offers an excellent walking trail, through the wooded hillsides and high plateaux of the Margeride, following mainly tracks, ancient *drailles* and paths. This stage can also be easily split into two days walking, with accommodation at the *gîte d'étape* of Le Sauvage, 24km after Paulhac. This will leave a walk of around 28km to Le Giraldès on the following day, most of which follows the Draille de la Margeride, GR43 trail.

STAGE 8
Le Giraldès to Bagnols-les-Bains

Distance	35.8km (22.2 miles)	**Ascent**	240m (787ft)
Off-road	81%	**Descent**	640m (2099ft)

Location	Distance (km)		Distance (miles)	
	Sectional	Cumulative	Sectional	Cumulative
LE GIRALDÈS (1300m)				
Lac de Charpal (1330m)	7.0	7.0	4.3	4.3
LAUBERT (1200m)	9.8	16.8	6.1	10.4
Larzalier	5.1	21.9	3.2	13.6
Carrefour de la Pierre-Plantée (1263m)	3.8	25.7	2.4	16.0
Le Felgeas	4.5	30.2	2.8	18.8
Château du Tournel (1100m)	1.3	31.5	0.8	19.6
Saint-Julien-du-Tournel (932m)	2.4	33.9	1.5	21.1
BAGNOLS-LES-BAINS (912m) [341/377]	1.9	**35.8**	1.1	**22.2**

A relatively short and fairly easy stage, with almost three times more descent than ascent, so allowing time to recover from the efforts of the last two days. The route is now leaving the Margeride as it heads ever south towards the high, rounded mountains of the Cévennes, which you will finally enter during the next stage.

Large, dammed Lac de Charpal is soon reached from Le Giraldès, and here the trail changes direction from south to southeast to head for the village of Laubert on Route National No. 88. There should be plenty of time for a long rest here, perhaps enjoying lunch in the restaurant (which is recommended).

After Laubert we finally leave the plateau behind, taking a long descent that passes the picturesque hamlet of Le Felgeas, after which the ruins of the Château

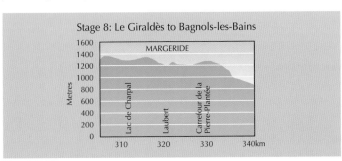

Stage 8: Le Giraldès to Bagnols-les-Bains

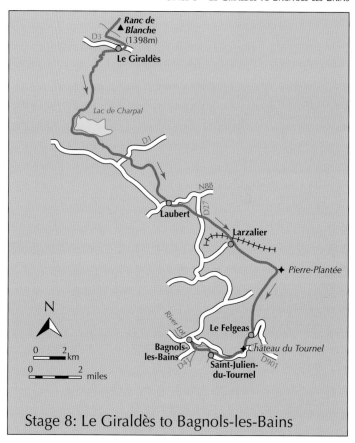

Stage 8: Le Giraldès to Bagnols-les-Bains

du Tournel are soon reached. Leave the bikes to explore these picturesque ruins on foot, but do take care, as they are old and possibly unsafe. (Do not venture past any notices prohibiting entry, which may have been erected since the author's visit.)

The last section into Bagnols-les-Bains is rather tedious and slow, over rough ground, but once you are there the large village has plenty of accommodation and places for refreshment, to prepare you for the following day into the hills to the south.

Facilities

A *gîte d'étape* and restaurant complex (Centre d'Accueil) is situated just outside the village of Laubert, a little after halfway through the stage. Popular with lorry drivers at lunchtime, the restaurant offers good-value food. The small town of Bagnols-les-Bains has cafés, restaurants, a choice of three hotels, a campsite and an *office de tourism*.

Places of Interest
Château du Tournel

The towers of this impressive ruined castle were built in the 12th century, at the same time as the village of Saint-Julien-du-Tournel, which it overlooks

Bagnols-les-Bains and 'Taking the Waters'

In the 17th century the spring waters of Bagnols-les-Bains were discovered to have health-giving properties, and the town developed to cater for the visitors who arrived in large numbers to 'take the cure'.

GTMC MOUNTAIN BIKE TRAIL

Leave the D3 in Giraldès on its southern side, cross a bridge and climb to the right, heading westwards and later to the southwest. On reaching a cross-tracks after a couple of kilometres, continue ahead on a forestry track towards the south. After a further 2km the main track veers to the right, to head southwest to reach the *barrage* of Lac de Charpal. You will need to lift your bike over the metal barriers at either end of this dam.

Soon leave the *barrage* road by turning left to follow the southern edge of the lake for about 2km, after which the track bears to the right – southeast – to head away from the lake. In a further 2.5km the trail crosses the D1. There will probably be a very wet and muddy surface for the next few hundred metres.

Remain on the track for about 3km. Just after a small quarry, turn right and follow the track as it descends into Laubert. For the *gîte d'étape*/restaurant/café complex (recommended) turn right for a few hundred metres, but to continue on the GTMC turn left on the N88 (care).

Just after the cemetery, leave this main highway by turning onto an ancient track. A direction of southeast is then maintained for about 8.5km, crossing first the D27 and a railway line, the latter near the hamlet of Larzalier. Make a right turn at the cross-tracks and menhir of Pierre-Plantée. Now maintain a southwesterly direction on another good track, gradually descending for 4km, before zigzags descend more steeply to the picturesque hamlet of Le Felgeas.

Turn right on the minor lane through the hamlet, and later take a track off to the left to descend very steeply (care) to the Château du Tournel. Leave your bike

Cycling through Le Felgeas

to explore these extremely picturesque ruins (care). Descend to the D901, emerging at the mouth of a road tunnel (take care). Turn right to head towards Bagnols. The easiest ride into the town is to remain on the D901, but the GTMC leaves it on the left after about 1.7km.

Descend to Saint-Julien-du-Tournel and cross the River Lot. Leave the village on a minor lane signposted to Oultet. At the bridge, climb to the right on a track that soon becomes a path. From here onwards to the outskirts of Bagnols, the going is very slow and difficult on a stony path. Eventually a road is reached – the GTMC climbs to the left here to reach the D41, but descend ahead to reach the centre of Bagnols-les-Bains.

ROAD BIKE ALTERNATIVE

See 'Stage Maps for the Road Bike Alternative', after the end of Stage 17.
Continue eastwards from Le Giraldès along the D3 to reach Châteauneuf-de-Randon. Head south along the D985 to l'Habitarelle on the N88. Here there are two alternatives, both of which, unfortunately, involve a ride on short sections of the N88 Langogne-to-Mende road, where special care is required.

The shorter alternative is to follow the N88 south for 5.5km to its junction with the D27. Alternatively, the much longer and harder, but more scenic route,

Resting by the Chateau du Tournel (Alan Sides)

first heads west, climbing along the D1 for about 9km to its junction with the D6, southeast of Lac de Charpal (for an optional visit to this lake, follow the D1 a few kilometres further westwards to the junction with the minor road that leads to the lake). Left along the D6 leads to the N88 near Laubert. Turn left on the N88 for 3km to reach the junction with the D27.

The D27 heads south to Allenc, and from there descends the valley west, then southwest, to reach the D901, 3km to the east of Bagnols-les-Bains. By turning left along the D901 you will soon reach your destination. 32km on the short route to the N88/D27 junction, or 43km on the long route to the N88/D27 junction, from Le Giraldès to Bagnols-les-Bains.

WALKING TRAIL – 2 DAYS

Again the GTMC forms a very good walking trail, with relatively little on roads. Laubert is the obvious place to spend the night, at the *gîte d'étape*/restaurant complex just outside the village. This gives a first day's walk of nearly 17km and a second day of 19km. The route for the walker is moderately easy, with relatively little ascent.

STAGE 9

Bagnols-les-Bains to Le Pont-de-Montvert

Distance	44.3km (27.5 miles)	**Ascent**	760m (2493ft)	
Off-road	64%	**Descent**	740m (2427ft)	

Location	Distance (km)		Distance (miles)	
	Sectional	*Cumulative*	*Sectional*	*Cumulative*
BAGNOLS-LES-BAINS (912m)				
Auriac (1180m)	3.9	3.9	2.4	2.4
La Croix de Maître-Vidal (1460m)	6.3	10.2	3.9	6.3
D20 (Mont Lozère)	12.8	23.0	8.0	14.3
Col de Finiels (1541m)	3.2	26.2	2.0	16.3
Le Cros (1340m)	6.5	32.7	4.0	20.3
Salarial	1.2	33.9	0.7	21.0
L'Hôpital	1.6	35.5	1.0	22.0
LE PONT-DE-MONTVERT (875m) [385.3/332.7]	8.8	**44.3**	5.5	**27.5**

The next two stages are the author's favourites, as the trail passes through the northern Cévennes, over the Mont Lozère massif to visit picturesque Le Pont-de-Montvert, from where it follows the highly scenic Bougès ridge to Florac, and then goes along the Tarn Gorges. This is Robert Louis Stevenson country, passing through the area where he undertook his celebrated 'Travels with a Donkey' in 1878.

Soon after leaving Bagnols the GTMC enters the Cévennes National Park for the first time. It remains within the park's boundaries for all of this stage, not leaving it until the final descent to Le Pont-de-Montvert. You will enjoy other large areas of the park in the days to come, as the route enters and exits on several

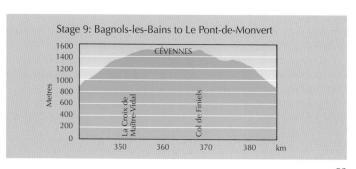

Stage 9: Bagnols-les-Bains to Le Pont-de-Monvert

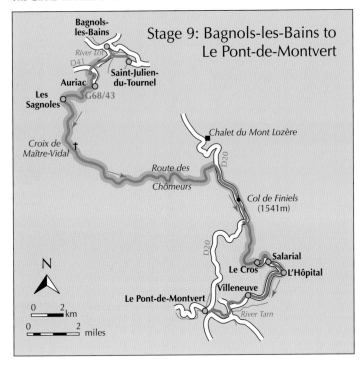

occasions, until you finally leave the Cévennes behind, just before Sauclières on Stage 13.

Today's route begins with a long and probably unwelcome climb of over 500m (1640ft) up onto the Mont Lozère massif, but once the ancient Croix de Maître-Vidal is reached, then wonderful off-road cycling follows, eastwards for many miles, all the way to the D20 that crosses Mont Lozère.

After an ascent to the Col de Finiels, care must then be taken on the very enjoyable descent from the col to not zoom past the small turning that leads to the trio of hamlets of Le Cros, Salarial and L'Hôpital.

Another very long and steep road descent takes the rider to Le Pont-de-Montvert – 'of bloody memory' (see below). Nowadays it is a very charming and romantic village, its old houses perched precariously on huge crags above the famed River Tarn, whose company we will often share on tomorrow's stage.

Facilities

Auriac has a small *gîte d'étape*, but those wanting refreshment at the halfway stage of the journey must make a 1.5km detour downhill on the D20 to the Chalet du Mont Lozère complex (Station du Mont Lozère), which consists of two hotel–restaurants, a *gîte d'étape* and a Cévennes National Park office. Drinks are also available here. There is a *chambres d'hôtes* in the tiny village of Finiels, again off-route, on the D20 south of the Col de Finiels. (If you stay at Finiels, you don't need to cycle back up the hill to rejoin the route of the GTMC, as Le Pont-de-Montvert is easily reached from Finiels by continuing on the D20, which leads directly to the village).

Le Pont-de-Montvert has accommodation of all types. There are three good hotels, a fine *gîte d'étape communal* housed in the Ecomuseum building complex and a campsite down by the River Tarn. There are plenty of shops, supermarkets, a *boulangerie*, restaurants, cafés and bars in the village, as well as a post office, bank, and a tourist office with a Cévennes National Park information centre.

Campers should note that wild camping is prohibited in the Cévennes National Park.

Places of Interest

Cévennes National Park

The second largest of France's national parks, the Parc National des Cévennes covers an area of 91,416 hectares. Created in 1970, the park occupies 0.5 per cent of France's landmass, but contains around 50 per cent of all the species of animals and plants that are to be found in France.

RLS and his 'Travels with a Donkey'

The Scottish author Robert Louis Stevenson, accompanied by his donkey Modestine, came this way in the autumn of 1878 on a 12-day pedestrian journey through the Velay and Cévennes from Le Monastier-sur-Gazeille to Saint-Jean-du-Gard. The book he wrote as a result, *Travels with a Donkey in the Cévennes*, has never since been out of print. Thousands of walkers and cyclists have followed in Stevenson's footsteps, a journey which today forms the basis of a thriving green tourist industry in the area.

Mont Lozère

The GTMC makes a complete west-to-east traverse of the huge massif of Mont Lozère. Its highest point, the Pic de Finiels at 1699m (5570ft), is also the highest peak in the whole of the Cévennes. A detour on foot to its summit on a clear day is very worthwhile, as the view is extensive and reaches as far as the Mediterranean.

Drailles

There are many ancient drove roads, or *drailles*, in the Cévennes, but very few indeed are now used to drive sheep or cattle along to market. These old tracks often provide the best and easiest biking and walking through the rugged, stony and scrub-covered hills. Drailles are particularly evident on Mont Lozère, where they are often marked with a line of standing stones, called *montjoies*, which date from the old droving days.

Le Pont-de-Montvert

A most picturesque Cévenol village located at the confluence of three rivers, the Tarn, Rieumalet and Martinet. There are many fine 16th-century houses built on rocks above the waters and along narrow winding streets, but the most attractive feature of the village is possibly the 17th-century humpback bridge over the River Tarn.

It was in Le Pont-de-Montvert that the War of the Camisards, between French Catholics and Protestants, broke out in 1702, when the Catholic governor, the Abbé du Chayla, was brutally murdered, in response to his violent suppression of the local Protestants. The guerrilla war continued until the Revolutionary Government of 1789 granted religious freedom to the French Protestants.

Old bridge and toll house, Le Pont-de-Montvert

Col de Finiels

GTMC MOUNTAIN BIKE TRAIL

Leave Bagnols on the D41, signposted to Lanuéjols. Soon after leaving Bagnols a road sign will be passed indicating that you are entering the Cévennes National Park. From hereon there are is no GTMC waymarking until Villeneuve, a few kilometres before Le Pont-de-Montvert, at the end of this stage.

Climb on the D41 to reach and take a minor road on the left that climbs steeply to the hamlet of Auriac. Here the surfaced lane gives way to unsurfaced tracks, following the line of the GR68/43 for the next few kilometres. The trail is also waymarked as a horse-riding trail (orange waymarks).

Climb on the trail to Les Sagnoles, where you turn sharply to the left and continue in a southerly direction for just under 3km to reach a cross-tracks – where the GR route continues ahead, but we turn left, following the sign to the Refuge du Mont Lozère. In 0.5km the prominent Croix de Maître-Vidal is reached. A stone cross has stood here in these uplands for many centuries, but the current one was restored in 1994.

There now follows what is perhaps the best and longest off-road section on the whole of the GTMC. The cycling is generally of an easy standard on good, firm tracks, and the views of the Mont Lozère massif are outstanding. From the cross head southeast, within 200 metres bearing left at a junction. This ancient, high-level unsurfaced road is now followed for many kilometres, all the way to the D20 road on Mont Lozère.

About 5.5km after leaving the Croix de Maître-Vidal you will come to a major junction. Take the left fork here, along the Route des Chômeurs, heading east. This leads in about 7km to the D20, the surfaced north–south road over Mont Lozère. These wanting refreshment should turn left, downhill to the Chalet du Mont Lozère complex.

The GTMC turns right. Follow the D20 uphill to the Col de Finiels (1541m) and remain on it for the first 1.4km of descent. Take special care not to miss the turning to the left, an easy thing to do when speeding downhill! A signpost 'DFCI La Baraquette' indicates the correct turning, sharply left downhill. This road/track soon heads to the south. About 3km after leaving the D20, turn left at a junction, now heading east towards the hamlet of Le Cros.

Follow the minor lane through a second hamlet, Salarial, to reach a third hamlet, l'Hôpital. Here turn very sharply down to the right to begin a long and steep descent on the surfaced road. Just before Villeneuve, the GTMC waymarking begins again at the boundary of the national park. This minor road emerges on the D20; turn left to enter Le Pont-de-Montvert.

ROAD BIKE ALTERNATIVE

See 'Stage Maps for the Road Bike Alternative', after the end of Stage 17.
This is a glorious ride in the divine countryside of the Cévennes, but there is plenty of climbing on the road over Mont Lozère. From Bagnols-les-Bains follow the D901 eastwards to Le Bleymard, a major staging post on the Robert Louis Stevenson Trail. From here take the mountain road, the D20, climbing south over Mont Lozére to the high point at the Col de Finiels – 1541m. A long and enjoyable descent leads via Prat Souteyrant to Le Pont-de-Montvert. 32km from Bagnols-les-Bains to Le Pont-de-Montvert.

WALKING TRAIL – 2 DAYS

From the hamlet of Auriac above Bagnols, there are two alternative walking routes. The GTMC can be followed to the Croix de Maître-Vidal and then on along the wide dirt road all the way to the point where the GTMC meets the D20 (and left along this road for 900 metres will lead to the *gîte d'étape* for an overnight at the Chalet du Mont Lozère complex, after a day's walk of around 24km).

Although this unsurfaced high road makes for excellent biking, with extensive views, walkers may find it a little too long and monotonous. But there is an excellent alternative route from Auriac. The GR68, the Tour du Mont Lozère, passes through the hamlet and can de followed eastwards via Oultet, Lozerette and Orcières to the large village of Le Bleymard, where there is a hotel and campsite.

Typical chaos boulders of the Cevennes

This would give a day-stage of about 14.5km. (This trail is included in the Cicerone guidebook *Walking in the Cévennes* by Janette Norton – see Appendix C).

On the following day, the Robert Louis Stevenson Trail provides an excellent walk of 19km, over the Pic de Finiels, at 1699m (5570ft) the highest point in the Cévennes, and down to the Le Pont-de-Montvert on the River Tarn. The route of the RLS Trail leaves the D20 after the Chalet du Mont Lozère complex, near the point where the GTMC reaches this road after its journey from the Croix de Maître-Vidal, so those walkers who have taken this alternative can join the RLS trail there. (A full route description of this stage of the RLS Trail is found in *The Robert Louis Stevenson Trail – the GR70*, see Appendix C).

The Cévennes offers more long-distance trails per square kilometre than probably anywhere else in France, so there are numerous other possibilities for walkers heading south. For example, from Auriac it is possible to follow the GR43/68 directly south to Florac via the Col des Faux, although this omits some of the best walking that the region has to offer, over the Pic de Finiels to Le Pont-de-Montvert and along the Bougès ridge.

From Florac the GR43 continues south to the Col des Faïsses, where it is met by the GR67, the Tour des Cévennes, which could then be followed further south to the Aire de Côte. From here the GR66, the Tour du Mont Aigoual, leads to the very summit of Mont Aigoual, where it joins the GTMC (Stage 12). The GRs 43, 68, 67 and 66 are all excellent trails that have been walked by the author, and are described in French Topo Guides (see Appendix C).

STAGE 10

Le Pont-de-Montvert to Sainte-Énimie

Distance	53.7km (33.4 miles)	Ascent	477m (1565ft)
Off-road	44%	Descent	726m (2381ft)

Location	Distance (km)		Distance (miles)	
	Sectional	Cumulative	Sectional	Cumulative
LE PONT-DE-MONTVERT (875m)				
L'Hermet	3.0	3.0	1.9	1.9
Col du Sapet (1080m)	7.5	10.5	4.6	6.5
Col de Perpau (989m)	4.2	14.7	2.6	9.1
Bédouès (Church) (590m)	7.1	21.8	4.4	13.5
Pont du Tarn (N106)	2.9	24.7	1.8	15.3
FLORAC (546m)	1.6	26.3	1.0	16.3
ISPAGNAC (518m)	9.7	36.0	6.0	22.3
Quézac (507m)	1.7	37.7	1.1	23.4
Castelbouc (521m)	9.2	46.9	5.7	29.1
Prades (536m)	1.1	48.0	0.7	29.8
SAINTE-ÉNIMIE (500m) [439/279]	5.7	**53.7**	3.6	**33.4**

The stage consists of two quite separate contrasting sections, before and after the town of Florac, firstly in the glorious rolling mountains of the Cévennes, and secondly following the dramatic course of one of France's most famous rivers, the Tarn.

The first half consists of a ride in the mountains, up to the Col du Sapet on the Bougès ridge, after which the GTMC follows the Stevenson Trail for a while,

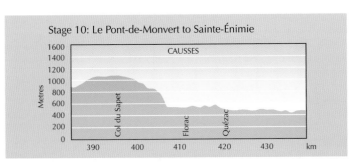

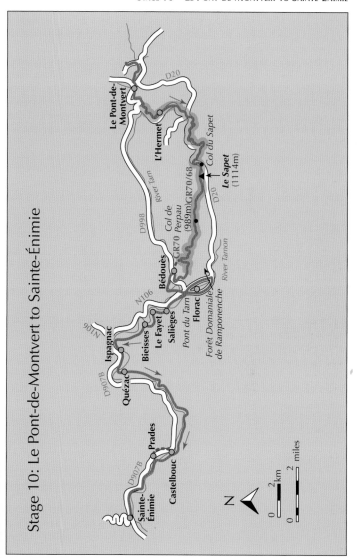

Stage 10: Le Pont-de-Montvert to Sainte-Énimie

before leaving it for a steep descent back down to the Tarn valley at the village of Bédouès. The route, although presenting some steep ups and downs at times, is relatively straightforward, with few problems of difficult terrain.

After a visit to Florac, possibly for lunch, the trail now follows the Tarn, as the river heads into the first of its main gorges. It crosses to the northern (right) bank of the river to visit the small town of Ispagnac, before re-crossing to the left bank to reach the smaller village of Quézac. The section of the GTMC from here is only recommended for experienced mountain bikers, and even these will almost certainly have to carry their bikes across some very steep and exposed sections above the river.

The far easier alternative is to cycle along the road that follows the northern or right bank of the river to the end of the stage at Sainte-Énimie. Whichever route you take, the spectacular River Tarn will be your companion for the afternoon. Enjoy its grandeur, because tomorrow you will say farewell to this sensational watercourse for the last time.

Facilities

Facilities are sparse between Le Pont-de-Montvert and Bédouès. Those prepared to make a 2.5km detour and long descent (with re-ascent the next day!) off the Bougès ridge to the south of the Col du Sapet will find a *gîte d'étape* in the hamlet of Mijavols. Bédouès has a café–restaurant, but for accommodation you will need to detour a couple of kilometres east along the D998 from Bédouès village to Cocurès, where there is a hotel–restaurant. Two campsites are in this vicinity, Camping Chantemerle at the Pont de la Pontèse below Bédouès, and Le Chon du Tarn camping to the southwest of Bédouès, north of Florac.

Florac has all the facilities you would expect of the largest town in the Cévennes. There are plentiful shops of most types, including several supermarkets, banks, a post office and a tourist office, and of course several restaurants, cafés and bars. The town has at least four hotels and two *gîtes d'étape*. The municipal campsite, La Tière, is by the river on the southern edge of the town.

Several campsites of various grades are situated along the Tarn valley between Florac and Castelbouc. Ispagnac has three hotels and an auberge, as well as several shops and a large supermarket. There are *chambres d'hôtes* in both Quézac and in Montbrun, the latter just a little off-route between Quézac and Castelbouc.

Tiny Prades has a hotel, and the large tourist village of Sainte-Énimie has plentiful shops selling both food and souvenirs. There are many cafés and restaurants in Sainte-Énimie, as well as several hotels, *auberges* and *chambres d'hôtes*, but note that accommodation in this popular area of the Tarn Valley can be heavily booked during the main summer season. Consult the tourist office in Sainte-Énimie if in doubt.

Places of Interest

Florac

A most attractive town situated at the foot of the high limestone cliffs of the Rocher de Rochefort, at the confluence of the Rivers Tarn, Tarnon and Mimente. It lies at a point where permeable limestone meets impermeable schists, and this leads to the reappearance of a subterranean stream, the Source de Pêcher, which flows through the centre of the town down a series of terraces. Many of the medieval streets are delightful, shaded by avenues of plane trees, with many old fountains, small bridges and narrow alleyways.

Tarn Gorges

The valley of the River Tarn is renowned for its spectacular gorges and historic villages. These include Ispagnac (ancient Ronanesque church), Quézac (Gothic church and naturally gassy mineral water) and Castelbouc (ruined château and picturesque village, with houses precariously clinging to the cliffs above the Tarn). More dramatic Tarn gorges lie to the west of the section followed by the GTMC (but can be followed on the Road Bike Alternative for Stage 11, see below).

Sainte-Énimie

Medieval Sainte-Énimie is today a popular centre for water sports, such as rafting, kayaking and canyoning. The church and museum are both worth a visit.

GTMC MOUNTAIN BIKE TRAIL

Cross the Pont-de-Tarn at Le Pont-de-Montvert. On the far side of the river, turn right following the minor road signposted to L'Hermet. After about 1.5km from Le Pont-de-Montvert you will re-enter the Cévennes National Park, so no more GTMC signs from now on, until a kilometre or so before Bédouès. Climb to pass through the hamlet of L'Hermet and remain on this pleasant lane all the way to the D20, 5.4km from Le Pont-de-Montvert.

Turn right along the D20 and follow it to the Col du Sapet. Here leave the road to take a broad track heading westwards, the GR70/68, to the north of Le Sapet (1114m) summit. Follow the main track, with good views to the north of the Mont Lozère plateau, to enter the Ramponenche Forest. Remain on this forest track for several kilometres.

Keep ahead on reaching a junction of seven tracks at the Col de Perpau (989m), slowly descending through the wood, later passing a small stone shelter on the left and later still the small Reservoir de la Chaumette, again on the left. Soon after this reservoir the track swings to head north and then reaches an important track junction. Turn left here to follow the GR68, leaving the GR70, which heads off downhill to the right.

Bike resting before the final descent into the Tarn Gorge (Alan Sides)

The trail heads southwesterly at first, then swings to the right to take a northerly direction. 1.2km after the GR68/70 junction, the GR68 goes left, signposted to Florac in 3.5km, but the GTMC continues ahead, signposted 'Florac 5km'. Descend steeply down to emerge in the village of Bédouès. The GTMC waymarks reappear while on this descent, as the trail leaves the national park.

Descend from the church in Bédouès to the D998. Turn left along this, soon leaving it by turning right on a minor lane, which crosses a bridge over the River Tarn. Turn left and follow the GTMC waymarks. The route passes through sections of open country and woodland, finally emerging on a lane that crosses the Tarn to reach the N106. Turn left (south) on this main road (care), and after about 600 metres turn right to cross the Pont de la Bessède over the River Tarnon, so entering the town of Florac.

After lunch and a stroll around this attractive town, leave Florac by first making your way to the town's *gendarmerie*, and from there following the road signposted to Salièges. At the road/track junction on leaving Salièges, fork right. Continue until just before the hamlet of Le Fayet, then bear to the left, soon climbing. At Bieisses the track becomes surfaced. Follow this, eventually descending to cross the River Tarn and enter the large village of Ispagnac.

A decision needs to be made at Ispagnac. There is a section of the GTMC, along the southeastern side of the river, after Quézac, which is difficult and possibly somewhat dangerous. The trail rises on an exposed narrow path above the river, and most people would need to carry bike and luggage over several of the more difficult rocky and steep sections. To avoid these difficulties, remain on the D907B, above the northwestern shore of the Tarn, all the way to Sainte-Énimie. Those who opt for this road route are, however, first recommended a short detour across the Tarn to Quézac, an attractive village nestling in a tight loop of the river.

Ride along Ispagnac's high street, leaving it to the left at its western end, to reach and cross another bridge over the Tarn, so returning to the south bank of the river. Follow the lane through picturesque Quézac, continuing ahead on a track that deteriorates to a narrow rocky path. Navigation is easy, but the terrain difficult, so progress is slow and care is required (see note above). Eventually the difficulties are over and the track becomes a surfaced lane heading towards Castelbouc. After this picturesque hamlet the trail deteriorates to a narrow path once more, passing through a wooded area.

Just over a kilometre after Castelbouc, the trail reaches a point opposite the village of Prades. Here use the concrete causeway to cross the River Tarn, so entering picturesque Prades. If, however, the river is in spate and water is covering the causeway, do not attempt a crossing. In this case return to Castelbouc and drop down through the hamlet to cross the Tarn on a road bridge. But if you have crossed the causeway at Prades, bear right to the Chemin du Moulin and then

Bleisses

steeply up the Chemin du Balat to the Place de l'Église. Continue up the Chemin du Balat to reach the D907B. Turn left along this road, entering Sainte-Énimie after 5km of easy cycling.

The GTMC officially remains on the southern, left bank of the River Tarn all the way from Castelbouc to Sainte-Énimie, although this route cannot be recommended, as it is rough, and many would have to carry their bikes over the more difficult sections.

ROAD BIKE ALTERNATIVE

See 'Stage Maps for the Road Bike Alternative', after the end of Stage 17.
An excellent ride eastwards along the Tarn Valley, through the Cévennes and down to Florac. The second half continues to follow the Tarn, but now alongside the dramatic gorges for which the river is justly famous.

The D998 is the tarmacked modern version of the track along the Tarn valley that Stevenson took on his celebrated travels in the Cévennes in 1878. Follow this road from Le Pont-de-Montvert to Florac, A few kilometres north along the N106 are unfortunately necessary to reach its junction with the D907B. Follow this road above the north bank of the Tarn through Ispagnac and on to Sainte-Énimie,

Travelling alongside the Tarn (Alan Sides)

below the high and huge limestone plateau of the Causses, which dominates the country to the south. A highly scenic ride. 48km from Le Pont-de-Montvert to Sainte-Énimie.

WALKING TRAIL – 2 DAYS

The obvious choice of route for the walker from Le Pont-de-Montvert to Florac is once again along the splendid RLS Trail. This section of the trail is considered by many to be its finest, climbing out of Le Pont-de-Montvert on an ancient but restored cobbled draille, and later following the spectacular Bougès ridge west towards Florac. It is, nevertheless, the longest of the RLS day stages, at 27.3km. (Full details in *The Robert Louis Stevenson Trail – the GR70*, see Appendix C).

The walker has a frustrating choice between Florac and Sainte-Énimie, choosing either the Tarn Gorges or a crossing of the limestone Causse to its south, both routes offering first-rate walking and landscape scenery.

The GTMC makes for an excellent walking trail of about 27km along the Tarn Valley, with relatively little road walking (remain on the southern, left bank, of the river, along the Sentier de la Vallée du Tarn, all the way from Castelbouc to Sainte-Énimie).

As an alternative to the river, the walker could take to the high limestone plateau of the Causse Méjean. Climb westwards out of Florac on the Tour du Causse Méjean, a GR de Pays, crossing the D16 and continuing via Le Tomple and Poujols to Chamblon. Leave the *tour* here to descend on the GR60 to Sainte-Énimie. This alternative gives a high-level walk of about 24km between the two towns, with a stiff ascent at the beginning of the day and a plunging descent back to the Tarn at its end.

STAGE 11
Sainte-Énimie to Cabrillac

Distance	38.7km (24.0 miles)	Ascent	991m (3251ft)
Off-road	23%	Descent	428m (1404ft)

Location	Distance (km)		Distance (miles)	
	Sectional	Cumulative	Sectional	Cumulative
SAINTE-ÉNIMIE (500m)				
Col de Coperlac (907m)	7.2	7.2	4.5	4.5
Mas-Saint-Chély (970m)	2.4	9.6	1.5	6.0
Le Buffre (935m)	4.6	14.2	2.9	8.9
Hures	4.1	18.3	2.5	11.4
Nivoliers (940m)	3.7	22.0	2.3	13.7
La Bégude-Blanche (ruins)	2.5	24.5	1.5	15.2
Serre de Capel (1156m)	2.2	26.7	1.4	16.6
Col de Perjuret (1030m)	4.8	31.5	3.0	19.6
Cabrillac (1194m)	6.6	38.1	4.0	23.6
GÎTE D'ÉTAPE DE CABRILLAC (1200m) [477.7/240.3]	0.6	**38.7**	0.4	**24.0**

Until the Cévennes was reached two days ago, long sections of the GTMC were through the immense forest that clothes a large area of the northern Massif Central. This has thinned somewhat over the last two stages, but today it does so more dramatically, as the trail heads up and then across the high limestone plateau known in French as the Causses. After a climb high up above the Tarn Gorges, you will turn your back on this marvellous river to begin a traverse of the Causse Méjean. Certainly there is still woodland, but much less of it than before, and you may be exposed to the rays of the sun for many hours, with little shelter from it, so be sure

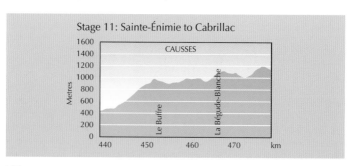

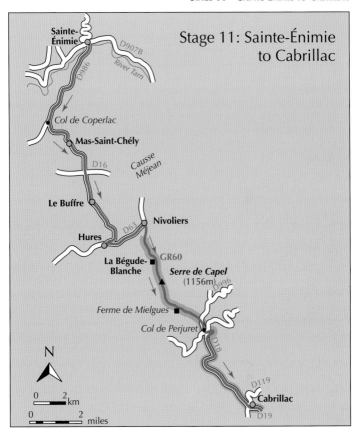

Stage 11: Sainte-Énimie to Cabrillac

to apply enough sunscreen and take plenty of water on your journey.

Today's route is in complete contrast to yesterday's. Much of it is on roads, but except for the climb out of Sainte-Énimie, and the road to Cabrillac from the Col de Perjuret (D roads which are also rarely busy with traffic), these are all quiet lanes across the Causses. A long and steep climb at the beginning of the day is bearable because of the quite amazing views down and over the Tarn Gorges.

At the Col de Coperlac, after an ascent of about 400m, the trail turns to the southeast to begin a traverse of Causse Méjean, first stop the pretty hamlet of Mas-Saint-Chély. After a possible refreshment stop here, the cycling is all easy and delightful as the GTMC passes through a succession of villages – Le Buffre, with its magnificent ancient cross, Hures and Nivoliers. In the latter, afternoon tea can be enjoyed in the relaxing atmosphere of the Chanet café–restaurant/*gîte d'étape*, sitting at their outside tables, enjoying the distant views of the Causses.

An off-road section follows, climbing to woods and up to the Serre de Capel. Then somewhat easier ground leads to the Col de Perjuret, where the route once again takes to the road for a climb up to Cabrillac and the *gîte d'étape* of that name. Although only open in July and August, do stay overnight here if you can, as it is one of the old traditional *gîtes d'étape*, in a wonderful location.

Facilities

Do food shopping in Sainte-Énimie at the beginning of the day, although bread and cakes can be bought at the village bakery in Mas-Saint-Chély. It is wise to buy food for the next two days, as the next good shop is not until Dourbies, at the end of Stage 12.

At a viewpoint before the Col de Coperlac, a small tourist shop and café are open in season. There is a hotel about 500 metres off-route, on the D986 after the Col de Coperlac.

At pretty Mas-Saint-Chély there is a café with cheap rooms (Chez Fages), as well as a hotel (Logis de France) with a restaurant, and a *chambres d'hôtes*. The *gîte d'étape*/café–restaurant called Le Chanet in the village of Nivoliers can be recommended. The gîte has rooms as well as the traditional dormitory.

Cabrillac *gîte d'étape* is not in the village itself, but situated in a charming rural spot, with good views over the surrounding hills, 600 metres south of the the village. Note that this *gîte d'étape* is open only in July and August, but a refuge room (abri) with beds/mattresses is left open at most other times. It is best to check by telephone before arriving, and if it is closed or full, a good alternative is Le Chanet *gîte d'étape* in Nivoliers, although this makes for a very long next day, unless a stop is made at Camprieu (see Stage 12), making up the distance to La Couvertoirade (see Stage 13) the day afterwards.

Yet another alternative, if Cabrillac *gîte d'étape* is closed and you have no tent, or do not wish to sleep in the *refuge* there, or need food, is to cycle from the Col de Perjuret west to the town of Meyrueis (hotel, *gîte d'étape* – and another at Marjoab, 2km further – and campsite), a distance of 11.5km. Return to the col the following morning to continue the route. (This option is not realistic for walkers.)

Alternatively, it is possible to head south after a night at Meyrueis or Marjoab, rejoining the route in the Camprieu/Saint-Sauveur/Gorges du Trévezel area, but this would omit a visit to the summit of Mont Aigoual, one of the highlights of this area.

View down to Saint-Chély-du-Tarn

Places of Interest

Col de Coperlac and the Tarn Viewpoint

Keep an eye out here for vultures circling overhead, riding the thermals above the Tarn.

Causse Méjean

South of the Tarn valley and to the west of Florac, this extensive, arid and stony limestone plateau rises abruptly to a height of over 1000m. Numerous tiny villages dot this landscape, which is ablaze with wildflowers in springtime.

Le Buffre: Croix du Buffre

The Croix du Buffre is considered one of the most beautiful carved stone crosses in Lozère.

Przewalski's Horses

The *petits chevaux de Przewalski* roam the area around Nivoliers and the La Bégude-Blanche ruin. This breed of small wild horses, originating in the Asian steppes of Mongolia, are thriving in this windswept upland plateau.

111

GTMC MOUNTAIN BIKE TRAIL

Climb out of Sainte-Énimie on the D986, heading southwest, above the eastern bank of the River Tarn. A long and steady hill climb, with outstanding views over the Tarn Gorges, follows on this road to the Col de Coperlac. A small café and tourist shop is passed at a viewpoint about a kilometre before the col.

Begin a ride across the high plateau of the Causse Méjean. Leave the main road at the col, turning left along the road that leads to Mas-Saint-Chély. Take the road heading southeast out of this pretty village. After 2.5km cross the D16 and continue south on the minor road, passing through Le Buffre (see its famous ancient cross) to reach Hures. Here turn left along the D63 to Nivoliers, passing through an area famous for its Mongolian horses.

At Nivolliers there is an opportunity for refreshment at the café/restaurant Le Chanet, then take the lane opposite this café, heading south. The trail almost immediately crosses into the Cévennes National Park, so GTMC waymarks disappear. After a cross the road becomes a track – be sure to take the path to the right, waymarked in red and white only a few hundred metres after leaving the village.

The GTMC follows the red and white markings of the GR60 from here to the Col de Perjuret. Climb on the trail and pass through a gate into the enclosure of the Przewalski's horses. (Caution: stay on the trail and do not approach these horses, as they may be dangerous.)

Interesting courtyard in Le Buffre

Wild horse country around Nivoliers and the Bégude-Blanche ruin

About 100 metres after going through a second gate, pass close to the ruins of the old farm of La Bégude-Blanche (make a short detour to the right to visit these ruins). The trail climbs steeply to the Serre de Capel (1156m).

The GTMC continues to the south and then the southeast to reach a cross-tracks close to the Ferme de Mielgues. Continue ahead to join and follow a minor lane to reach the Col de Perjuret at the D996, at its junction with the D18. Follow the latter road, heading south.

Climb on this road for just over 6.5km to reach the minor road into the pretty hamlet of Cabrillac. Ride south through this settlement to return to the D18 at its junction with the D19. Take the latter, which is coincident with the GR66, heading southeast. After about 600 metres turn left, downhill, to reach the *gîte d'étape*.

ROAD BIKE ALTERNATIVE

See 'Stage Maps for the Road Bike Alternative', after the end of Stage 17.
Two alternative routes are possible. The most direct of these involves firstly a climb on the D986, south from Sainte-Énimie, following the mountain bike route to the Col de Coperlac, and then continuing on this road across the western edge of the Causse Méjean to drop down to the attractive little town of Meyrueis. From here turn left to head west on the D996 to the Col de Perjuret, where you rejoin the

mountain bike route, to head south on the D18 to Cabrillac. This is an excellent cycle ride in beautiful countryside. 48km from Sainte-Énimie to Cabrillac.

The more spectacular, but considerably longer option, is to follow the River Tarn on its journey southwest and then south to Le Rozier, along the dramatic Gorges du Tarn. From Sainte-Énimie take the D907B along the northern shore of the Tarn. Pass through La Malène, after which, below the Point Sublime viewpoint, the river and its following road change direction to head south, reaching the Jonte valley at Le Rozier (*gîte d'étape*). Now head east up this valley on the D996, through the Gorges de Jonte, all the way to Meyrueis (accommodation), where the route described above is joined and followed to Cabrillac.

It is probably best to stay the night in Meyrueis rather than go on to Cabrillac, unless a bed has been booked in the Cabrillac *gîte d'étape*. This is one of the great rides of this southern corner of France, and highly recommended. It is 76km from Sainte-Énimie to Cabrillac on this route.

WALKING TRAIL – 1 DAY

The walker should cross the Tarn at Sainte-Énimie and leave the D986 after a few hundred metres by taking the GR60 heading south across the Causses to the hamlets of Chamblon and Le Fraisse, and on to Nivoliers, where the GTMC and the GR60 are coincident.

The GR60 follows the D18 from the Col de Perjuret, but after about 1.5km leaves it for an off-road section of a couple of kilometres before rejoining the D18 a little before it enters Cabrillac. This walk on the GR60 from Sainte-Énimie to the *gîte d'étape* near Cabrillac is about 30km, and more direct than the GTMC.

STAGE 12
Cabrillac to Dourbies

Distance	49.5km (30.7 miles)	**Ascent** 895m (2936ft)
Off-road	64%	**Descent** 1185m (3887ft)

Location	Distance (km)		Distance (miles)	
	Sectional	Cumulative	Sectional	Cumulative
Gîte d'étape de Cabrillac (1200m)				
Mont Aigoual (1565m)	9.5	9.5	5.9	5.9
Col de Prat-Peyrot	3.5	13.0	2.2	8.1
Col de la Caumette (1455m)	1.9	14.9	1.2	9.3
La Croix de Fer (1178m)	4.8	19.7	3.0	12.3
North of CAMPRIEU (1100m)	0.8	20.5	0.5	12.8
Saint-Sauveur (960m)	4.1	24.6	2.5	15.3
D157	3.4	28.0	2.1	17.4
Comeiras (940m)	6.3	34.3	3.9	21.3
Canayère (890m)	5.5	39.8	3.4	24.7
Col de Rhodes (D151) (922m)	3.6	43.4	2.2	26.9
DOURBIES (897m) [527.2/190.8]	6.1	**49.5**	3.8	**30.7**

A grand stage, but a long one, and not exactly easy, although the severity of the day will be greatly reduced if you take the much easier road option to the summit of Mont Aigoual.

The official route of the GTMC from the Gîte de Cabrillac is firstly over some very rough ground, and then there is a very steep climb (most people will be pushing their bikes!) on a stony track/path. It is all pretty steep and rough going with a mountain bike (walkers will have little difficulty) and care with navigation is required.

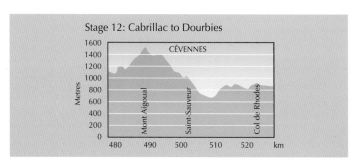

Stage 12: Cabrillac to Dourbies

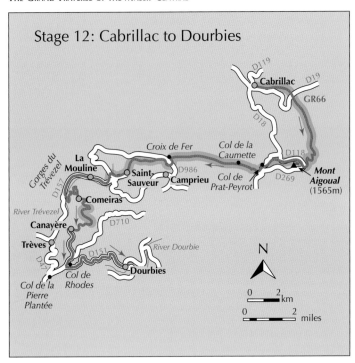

Stage 12: Cabrillac to Dourbies

Whichever route you decide to take, you will surely enjoy the view from the observatory on the summit of the highest peak in the southern Cévennes, 1565m (5133ft) above sea level. It matters little that there is a car park here, and that you will no doubt be sharing the top with many tourists – Mont Aigoual is still a marvellous viewpoint.

There follows a few miles of easy cycling, first on road to the Col de Prat-Peyrot and then good forest tracks past the Col de la Caumette, but the route to the Croix de Fer is far from easy, on a very confined, steep trail. More off-road cycling after the outskirts of Camprieu leads to the church at Saint-Sauveur, before much easy cycling, downhill on road alongside the Trévezel Gorges, before another steep uphill section on a minor road to the village of Comeiras.

The route from here to the next village, Canayère, is along an ancient balcony path, which offers stunning views down to the Gorges du Trévezel, but it is far from easy, and most riders will be pushing their bikes. Special care must be taken on one very steep section down to cross a stream, and then very steeply back up the other side, but all difficulties are over by the time Canayère is reached, where the trail becomes a track and then a road to the Col de Rhodes. From there it is downhill all the way to Dourbies, where you can spend the night at the super, traditional *gîte d'étape* next to the village church.

Facilities

A café and overnight *refuge* are located on the very summit of Mont Aigoual, by the observatory building. Even if you are not staying overnight at this marvellous high viewpoint, the café is most welcome after the long, hard climb to the summit.

Camprieu has a hotel and nearby *gîte d'étape*, as well as a campsite, while at tiny Saint-Sauveur there is only a Cévennes National Park office.

A little before the entrance to the village of Dourbies there is the Maison de Dourbies, a *maison de vacances*. This large establishment offers accommodation to overnighters as well as those staying longer.

The *gîte d'étape* in Dourbies, a traditional gem, is by the church in the centre of this lovely village. Nearby there is a combined café–restaurant and *épicerie*, and it is here that enquiries about the *gîte d'étape* should be made. Hospitality is first-rate, and if you do not wish to prepare your own meal in the *gîte*, then dinner in this village restaurant is of a high quality and superb value.

Table d'orientation on Mont Aigoual

Places of Interest
Mont Aigoual
The highest peak in the southern Cévennes, Mont Aigoual (1565m, 5133ft) has a meteorological observatory on its very summit. Built in 1887, data from its weather station over the years has recorded wind speeds of up to 250km/hour and annual rainfall of 220cm.

The view from the summit is very extensive indeed on a clear day, and a *table d'orientation* on the roof of the observatory allows you to identify the surrounding hills and valley systems.

Gorges du Trévezel and Gorges de la Dourbies
Percolating water through limestone has gouged out, over aeons of time, these two deep and spectacular gorge systems, near to the tranquil village of Dourbies in the Southern Cévennes.

GTMC MOUNTAIN BIKE TRAIL

The off-road section from the Cabrillac *gîte d'étape* to the summit of Mont Aigoual is a very demanding mountain bike trail, over very rough terrain at times, very steep, occasionally overgrown, and waymarks tend to be sparse in places. The much easier option is to climb the mountain on the D18 (NB not the D19), bearing left near the top on the D118 to the summit car park. This is an enjoyable hill climb to one of southern France's most notable summits.

If you do decide to take the mountain bike route, then don't return to the D19, but head straight out of the *gîte d'étape*, eastwards on the GR66 (red and white waymarks). Follow the waymarks to cross the D19 after 2km (bikes may need to be to be carried at times over rough and rocky ground). The climb now begins in earnest, on a stony track/path southeastwards, steeply over open ground at first, but soon entering woodland.

After about 1.5km ignore the GR route, which takes a stile on the left, instead continuing ahead on the stony track through the trees. Eventually you reach a wide track on your left at a clearing. Continue ahead on this to reach a road, the D269, at a bend, a little below and 600 metres to the east of Mont Aigoual's summit. Bear right on this road to ride to the summit car park.

After a visit to the summit complex, descend westwards on the D118 towards the Col de Prat-Peyrot. When the D118 bends sharply to the right, take the track ahead (GR66 and GR6) – this descends to join another road, the D18, which you follow to the col. At the col, where there is a ski station, the GR66 and GR6 separate. The GR66 heads southwest, but ignore this, instead taking the GR6 along a forest track signposted to Marjoab.

Hillside close to Cabrillac

After 1.5km, at the Col de la Caumette, there is a second bifurcation of GR trails. Ignore the GR6A heading northwest, but continue ahead along the track, following the GR6 westwards. After a further 1.5km leave the forest track by taking a path on the left, still on the GR6. Remain on this trail, a narrow, rough and very steep path, heading westwards all the way to the Croix de Fer, where you will meet a metalled lane. Turn left on this, descending, and note the first GTMC waymark since Nivoliers on Stage 11.

Follow the waymarks to cross the D986 (or turn left on this road if you need the facilities of Camprieu). Turn right at a junction, following the GR trail (the GTMC waymarks soon disappear again as the route re-enters the national park).

Follow the trail signposted to Aigue-Bonne and Saint-Sauveur. The narrow path twists and turns in the woodland, but the way should never be in doubt as the trail contours westwards, eventually turning south to reach a narrow lane at Saint-Sauveur (church and national park office). Descend westwards on this minor road to reach the D157, the GTMC signs soon reappearing. Follow this road descending towards La Mouline.

Easy and pleasant cycling takes you down through La Mouline to the Gorges du Trévezel. About 2.8km after La Mouline be sure to leave the D157 by crossing a bridge over the Trévezel river and climbing on the hairpinned minor road to Comeiras. (Anyone wanting to avoid the next cross-country section should stay on the D157 to Trèves, then take the D47 to the Col de la Pierre Plantée, where a sharp turn to the northeast leads along the D151 to Dourbies.)

Welcome sign for the gîte d'étape

At the first houses of the hill-top hamlet, take a path on the left (this trail, often narrow and tree covered, is also used by horse riders, so especial care is required). After about a kilometre the Cévennes National Park is re-entered, so there are no GTMC signs for a while. The ground is rough, with occasional very steep sections, particularly one over a stream, and so care is required.

About 2.2km after leaving Comeiras take the track climbing on the left, the cycling soon becoming much easier as the national park is exited (GTMC signs recommence), and the track leads to the hamlet of Canayère.

Turn left in Canayère on a lane that leads to the D710. Turn right along this road to reach the Col des Rhodes at the junction with the D151. Turn left along the D151 to enjoy easy cycling, with good views all the way, finally descending to Dourbies.

ROAD BIKE ALTERNATIVE

See 'Stage Maps for the Road Bike Alternative', after the end of Stage 17.
For those who relish hill climbs, this is your day! The figures speak for themselves: Cabrillac is at an altitude of 1194m, whereas Mont Aigoual stands proud over the southern Cévennes at a height of 1565m, the highest point on the GTMC – so an ascent of 371m (1217ft) starts the day. The climb on the D18 to the summit of

Mont Aigoual is generally well graded, and should present no particular difficulty for the cyclist who, by now, should be well used to the hilly terrain of the Massif Central. The view from the summit is certainly worth all the effort to reach it.

High-quality cycling continues for the rest of the day. Follow the D269 to the Col de Prat-Peyrot, and then southwards to the Col de la Sereyrède (1299m). From here follow the D986 westwards to Camprieu, where you pick up the D157 continuing west, then south along the Gorges du Trévezel to Trèves. Continue south on the D47 to the Col de la Pierre Plantée, where a sharp turn to the northeast leads along the D151 to Dourbies. 47km from Cabrillac to Dourbies.

WALKING TRAIL – 2 TO 3 DAYS

The walker has two GR trails to chose from to reach Mont Aigoual. The more direct is the GR60, although this reaches the mountain a kilometre or so to the west of the summit, so you would need to retrace your steps after a visit to the observatory and summit viewpoint.

The recommended trail is the GR66, the Tour du Mont Aigoual, which first heads eastwards from Cabrillac to cross the D19 at Le Caumel, and then southeast via the Col de l'Estrade to the Aire de Côte (*gîte d'étape*), 11km from Cabrillac. From here it climbs to the west to reach the summit of Mont Aigoual in another 7km , where accommodation for the night may be obtained in the *refuge*.

The GR66 continues via the Col de Prat-Peyrot, where it leaves the GTMC to head south via the Col de la Serreyrède to l'Espérou, where there is a *gîte d'étape*, 6.5km after Mont Aigoual. From l'Espérou it is a further 25km on the GR66 via the Col des Portes and the Col de l'Homme Mort to Dourbies.

Another alternative is to head east on the GR62 from the Col de la Serreyrède to Camprieu, close to the GTMC, and from there follow the GR66A south-south-west to the point where it meets the GR66 north of Dourbies, and follow this GR into the village.

Yet another alternative is to remain on the GTMC, which is coincident with the GR6 from the Col de Prat-Peyrot to the Croix de Fer, and from there either continue on the GTMC (not particularly recommended, as there is considerable road walking from there to Dourbies), or preferably, follow the GR66A and 66 to Dourbies as described above.

STAGE 13

Dourbies to La Couvertoirade

Distance	44.7km (27.8 miles)	**Ascent**	758m (2486ft)
Off-road	56%	**Descent**	818m (2683ft)

Location	Distance (km)		Distance (miles)	
	Sectional	*Cumulative*	*Sectional*	*Cumulative*
DOURBIES (897m)				
Prunaret	4.1	4.1	2.5	2.5
Pratlac (1072m)	0.8	4.9	0.5	3.0
Col de la Combe (924m)	19.1	24.0	11.9	14.9
Col de la Barrière (808m)	2.5	26.5	1.6	16.5
SAUCLIÈRES (720m)	3.8	30.3	2.3	18.8
Gaillac	7.1	37.4	4.4	23.2
D55 (east of Cazejourdes) (758m)	2.6	40.0	1.6	24.8
LA COUVERTOIRADE (776m) [571.9/146.1]	4.7	**44.7**	3.0	**27.8**

Today is a transitional day, where our route has one more stretch through the wooded hills of the southern Cévennes, before finally dropping down to lower open country, where there is very much a Mediterranean feel – an indication that you are now embarking on the last stages of this traverse of the Massif Central.

The route is much easier than the previous stage, but almost as long, with nearly as much ascent, and any errors in navigation in the woods between Pratlac and the Col de la Combe would waste a lot of time. The latter stages, from the Col de la Barrière via Sauclières to La Couvertoirade, are relatively straightforward.

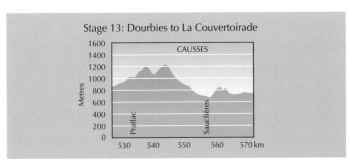

Stage 13: Dourbies to La Couvertoirade

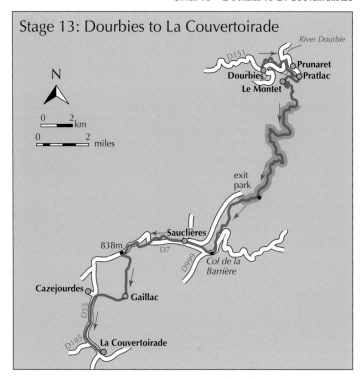

Stage 13: Dourbies to La Couvertoirade

The day begins with a road section west along the Dourbies valley, before a climb up to the hamlets of Prunaret, Pratlac and Le Montet, each one progressively higher in the hills. At the last of these hamlets we leave the road to take to a series of forest rides and tracks. The terrain is not particularly difficult to negotiate, but concentration with navigation is essential, as we have, for the very last time, re-entered the Cévennes National Park, so GTMC signs are absent until after the Col de la Combe.

Follow the route description carefully and you will exit the woods at the correct point, before reaching the D999 and following this road westwards into the village of Sauclières. From here be sure to apply plenty of sunscreen if it is a sunny day, as there is little shade until the ancient walled town of La Couvertoirade at the end of the day – a magical place to spend the night (once most of the tourists have left).

Facilities

Buy enough food for a few days from the *épicerie* in Dourbies. There is a grocery shop in Sauclières and a *gîte-auberge*, Le Mas-Bresson, in Le Prunaret, but after that there are no facilities until after leaving the national park and descending to the D999 in the valley to the south. A detour from the GTMC from the Col de la Combe leads to the village of Alzon, where there is a *gîte d'étape*. Also, as well as the *épicerie*, Sauclières has a restaurant and post office.

A *gîte d'étape* is part of the *centre équestre* in Gaillac, southwest of Sauclières, but the most atmospheric place to stay is inside the walled town of La Couvertoirade. The Gîte de la Cité occupies an old traditional house in the town, and is a pleasant place to spend the evening.

La Couvertoirade is an extremely touristy place, with many cafés, tourist shops and restaurants (with tourist menus), but there is no *épicerie*. Once the day visitors have left, these establishments tend to close, so be sure to book your evening meal in the *gîte d'étape* if you don't want to prepare your own food (which in any case will have to be carried in from Dourbies or Sauclières).

From here onwards there are few campsites until the Mediterranean coast is reached south of Montpellier.

Places of Interest
La Couvertoirade

Founded in the 12th century, this fortified town, home to the medieval Knights Templars, is still enclosed by intact towers and high walls. Although a seething mass of tourists during the day, by early evening most of these have departed. An overnight stay allows the visitor to soak up the atmosphere of this very special place.

GTMC MOUNTAIN BIKE TRAIL

Leave Dourbies on the D151, direction L'Espérou, initially heading north. After 2.6km turn right on the D299b, crossing the River Dourbie and climbing to the hillside hamlet of Prunaret. Continue on the road passing another hamlet, Pratlac, to arrive at a third hamlet, Le Montet. From here take the route forestière in the direction of the Col de l'Homme Mort. This forest road twists and turns for about 2.5km to reach the boundary of the Cévennes National Park (so no GTMC way-marks for here on) at a track junction.

Leave the *route forestière* to take another track on the right, signposted 'Chemin Forestière No. 152'. After about 750 metres you reach a junction of three tracks – take the middle of these three trails. After about 3km, at a Y-junction of tracks, take the right, lower fork. Later this trail bends to the right over a roughly surfaced concrete bridge, then follows a stream on the right for a while.

Pratlac, where the metalled road ends

Reach a sign for Forest Road nos. 155 and 154. Continue ahead on no.155, soon bearing northwest and climbing to a junction of tracks at a small clearing. Here turn very sharply to the left, remaining on this main track, ignoring a few minor tracks on the way. Eventually join route no. 159 and keep ahead on this at a small concrete building, joining the GR66, with its red and white waymarks. Climb to a track junction where our route leaves the GR66.

Continue in the same direction, but now following Chemin Forestière no. 79. Soon reach a junction of four tracks. Turn right here, taking forest road no. 77. Follow this track, generally in a southwesterly direction, joining the GR71 after about 2km, and continue for several kilometres more, descending to the Col de la Combe.

Continue ahead here, soon exiting the Cévennes National Park for the last time (GTMC signs reappear), and cycle down to the D999 at the Col de la Barrière. Turn right on the D999 to head westwards towards Sauclières. In 3km, at the junction with the D7, turn right on the D999, pass under a bridge, and then immediately turn left up a cobbled path into the village of Sauclières.

After a visit to the village, descend southwestwards to meet the D7. Head west-southwest, following waymarks, to take a track to the right (north) of the D7, rejoining the road again in less that a kilometre. Turn right on the road, but after about 100 metres, at a sharp right bend in the road, leave the D7 again to follow a track on the left to the west-southwest. After about 600 metres this swings to the

Horses at the riding school at Gaillac

north to climb back up to the D7. Rejoin this road, and turn left along it for about a kilometre to an unnamed col at map spot height 838m.

Turn sharp left off the road at this point, initially heading east, but after 500 metres bearing right to head south towards Gaillac. This trail passes through several gated fenced fields. Near the equestrian centre at Gaillac follow the minor road to the right, which leads after 2km to the main D55. Turn left on this road, cycling south to the junction with the D185. Turn left here to enter the walled village of La Couvertoirade.

ROAD BIKE ALTERNATIVE

See 'Stage Maps for the Road Bike Alternative', after the end of Stage 17.

Once again there are two alternatives. The most direct route between Dourbies and La Couvertoirade is to return to the Col de la Pierre Plantée, and from there descend south on the D341 to Saint-Jean-du-Bruel. Head west from here, on the D999, to visit Nant, before turning south on the D55 to reach the D7. Continue south on the D55 to reach La Couvertoirade. 39km from Dourbies to La Couvertoirade.

The alternative is a much longer and harder route, but it samples some of the best countryside in the southern Cévennes. Head westwards from Dourbies on the D151, as for the mountain bike route, but remain on this road for about 13km

Shadows in the street, La Couvertoirade

until it meets the D48 southwest of l'Espérou. Follow this scenic road southwards over the Col du Minier and on via Arphy to the town of Le Vigan.

Cross the D999, still following the D48, south to Montdardier. From here it is possible to take a direct route to La Vacquerie et St-Martin-de-Castries (end of Stage 14) by continuing south on the D48, via Le Cros to Madièries, and from there cycling on the D25 via Saint-Maurice-Navacelles to La Vacquerie et St-Martin-De-Castries, 27km from Montdardier.

However, to reach La Couvertoirade you must turn at Montdardier to head westwards along a series of minor roads. The D113 leads to Blandas, a few kilometres after which it reaches the D813. Turn left along this road to Vissec, continuing on the D113B to Le Camp d'Alton and then the D142 to Sorbs. Continue on the D142 through Le Cros to meet the D9 southeast of Le Caylar. From this village head north, first on the D9 and later on the D55 to La Couvertoirade. 85km from Dourbies to La Couvertoirade.

WALKING TRAIL – 2 DAYS

From Dourbies there is initially a choice. Either take the GR66 south out of the village, via La Rouvière and Ressançon to join the GTMC about 7km after leaving Dourbies. Alternatively, follow the GTMC to the point where it meets the GR66, although this is longer and involves an initial 6km kilometres of road walking. Then follow the GTMC/GR71 to the Col de la Combe and down to the Col de la Barrière.

You may need to make a detour to the village of Alzon for overnight accommodation in its *gîte d'étape* (a track leads there directly from the Col de la Combe). The GR71 continues to Campestre-et-Luc, where there is a chambres-d'hôtes, before turning to the southeast to pass through Le Luc and then approach La Couvertoirade from the east.

Alternatively, follow the GTMC from the Col de la Barrière to Sauclières and on to Gaillac, so entering La Couvertoirade from the north, but note that this option involves quite a lot of road walking.

STAGE 14

La Couvertoirade to La Vacquerie et St-Martin-de-Castries

Distance	31.1km (19.3 miles)	Ascent	263m (863ft)
Off-road	75%	Descent	415m (1361ft)

Location	Distance (km)		Distance (miles)	
	Sectional	*Cumulative*	*Sectional*	*Cumulative*
LA COUVERTOIRADE (776m)				
Le Cros (740m)	6.8	6.8	4.2	4.2
Saint-Michel (770m)	3.2	10.0	2.0	6.2
La Vernède	5.2	15.2	3.2	9.4
Saint-Pierre-de-la-Fage (620m)	5.3	20.5	3.3	12.7
Col de Jouquet (769m)	2.5	23.0	1.6	14.3
Col du Vent (700m)	4.3	27.3	2.6	16.9
LA VACQUERIE ET ST-MARTIN-DE-CASTRIES (630m) [603/115]	3.8	**31.1**	2.4	**19.3**

Fit and experienced mountain bikers could accomplish the next two stages to Saint-Jean-de-Fos in one day, but this part of the route has been split into two stages in this guidebook for several reasons.

Unless an extremely early start is made from La Couvertoirade, the Col de Vent will not be reached until the sun is high in the sky, by which time the very steep climb to Saint-Baudille mountain would be most exhausting in the heat of the afternoon. Also, if the two stages were combined there would be little time to visit the recommended, picturesque and historic village of Saint-Guilhem-le-Désert (see Stage 15). So better to take it easy, enjoy the journey, and while away

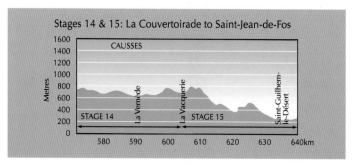

Stages 14 & 15: La Couvertoirade to Saint-Jean-de-Fos

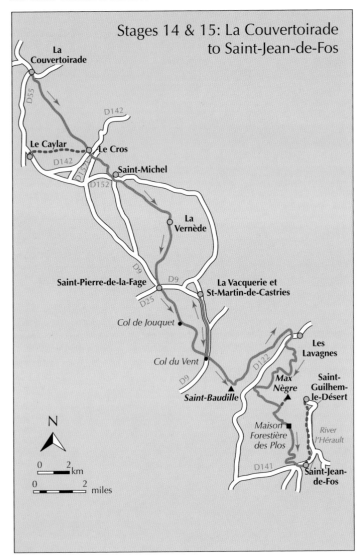

Stages 14 & 15: La Couvertoirade to Saint-Jean-de-Fos

a pleasant afternoon in the tranquil backwater of La Vacquerie et St-Martin-de-Castries. The village may be small, but it has a very long official title – most locals, fortunately, refer to it simply as La Vacquerie.

The route heads in a straight line southeast from La Couvertoirade, reaching firstly the hamlet of Le Cros, which has a medieval cross adorned with a primitive stone-carved Christ. You then move on to Saint-Michel, a village with the ruins of a château on the hillside above. Neither of these settlements has even a simple café.

The tracks taken across the Causses are rough and stony, but otherwise the route is without difficulty. After the few old buildings of La Vernède the trail changes direction, now heading south to reach the D9 at the village of Saint-Pierre-de-la-Fage, which is also café-less.

The shortest and easiest route from here is to turn left to cycle the few miles into La Vacquerie. But the GTMC, rarely taking an easy alternative, takes to the low hills to the southeast, with more off-road work on rough, stony tracks until the Col du Vent, 'windy pass', is reached, from where a left turn leads downhill on the road to La Vacquerie.

Again there is little possibility of shade on today's ride, so the wise will take suitable precautions against the fierce sun, as well as enough water to last the distance. The village of La Vacquerie is a very pleasant place to while away a hot afternoon. There are short local rambles waymarked around the village.

Facilities

There is no opportunity for refreshment between La Couvertoirade and La Vacquerie, so the water tap in Saint-Michel may be a welcome sight if the day is hot. La Vernède has a basic *relais d'étape*, but the building was locked and looked deserted at the time of the author's visit.

La Vacquerie has a hotel–restaurant (L'Auberge des Causses-le-Zibardie – recommended) and a CAF *refuge*, opposite each other in the centre of the village, and also a *gîte d'étape*. There are no shops in the village, but a mobile shop visits on some afternoons, or the hotel may be able to sell you some food.

Places of Interest
Le Cros
Don't miss the interesting ancient cross at the tiny village of Le Cros.

Saint-Michel
Striking ruins of a château look down on the peaceful village of Saint-Michel.

GTMC MOUNTAIN BIKE TRAIL

Leave La Couvertoirade passing through its ramparts and heading southeast. Follow the waymarked trail which reaches, in just under 3km, a cross-tracks. Continue ahead at this point, still travelling in a southeasterly direction, all the way to Le Cros. Just before reaching the village you pass an ancient cross on the left-hand side of the track.

At Le Cros the GTMC meets the GT34, the Grande Traversée de l'Hérault, which has entered the village from Le Caylar in the west. From this point the GTMC and GT34 are coincident until the end of Stage 15. The GT34 is waymarked very distinctively on short green metal posts, and it is these that you should follow until Saint-Jean-de-Fos.

Cross the D142 in Le Cros, pass alongside the village cemetery and cross a second road, the D152E. Continue southeast, eventually descending to the D152 to the west of Saint-Michel. Turn left on this road to enter Saint-Michel.

Leave the village on the road signposted to Soulagets, but turn right off it after about 300 metres, onto a track resuming a southeasterly direction. Follow the waymarks at track junctions, maintaining direction to reach a minor surfaced lane after about 4km. Turn right along this to reach the farm of La Vernède.

Cycle through the hamlet to take a track on the right that heads in a generally southerly direction, to reach in just over 4km the D9. Turn left on this to enter the hamlet of Saint-Pierre–de-la-Fage. Cross the D25/D9 at a roundabout and follow the main track to the southeast for 2.5km to the Col de Jouquet. Continue to the

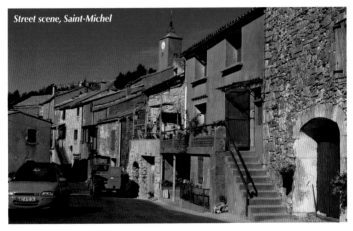

Street scene, Saint-Michel

Windmill outside Saint-Pierre-de-la-Fage

left, and when the track becomes a tarmacked minor road, do not follow this, but take the track to the right and follow it to the D9 at the Col du Vent.

The GTMC crosses the road here to continue ahead towards the hills. However, to spend the night in the pleasant village of La Vacquerie, turn left (north) along the road to descend for almost 4km to enter the village.

ROAD BIKE ALTERNATIVE

See 'Stage Maps for the Road Bike Alternative', after the end of Stage 17.
A simple and short ride takes the road cyclist to the end of this stage. From La Couvertoirade retrace your route back to Le Caylar along the D55 and D9, and from there continue on the D9 southeastwards to reach Saint-Pierre-de-la-Fage. Here take the main road, D25, eastwards to La Vacquerie. 25km from La Couvertoirade to La Vacquerie et St-Martin-De-Castries.

As this is such a short distance, you may want to combine this route with the Stage 15 road route, still giving a total distance of only 47km.

WALKING TRAIL – 1 DAY

Stage 14 of the GTMC is a pleasant and easy walking route, albeit a fairly long one, with little ascent or descent. This stage can be shortened by about 6km by following the main road (D25) eastwards from Saint-Pierre-de-la-Fage, directly to La Vacquerie, rather than walking via the Col de Jouquet and the Col du Vent.

STAGE 15

La Vacquerie et St-Martin-de-Castries to Saint-Jean-de-Fos

Distance	37.5km (23.3 miles)	Ascent	620m (2034ft)
Off-road	59%	Descent	1030m (3378ft)

Location	Distance (km)		Distance (miles)	
	Sectional	*Cumulative*	*Sectional*	*Cumulative*
LA VACQUERIE ET ST-MARTIN-DE-CASTRIES (630m)				
Col du Vent (700m)	3.8	3.8	2.4	2.4
D122	8.0	11.8	5.0	7.4
South of Max Nègre	8.8	20.6	5.4	12.8
SAINT-JEAN-DE-FOS (100m)	7.7	28.3	4.8	17.6
SAINT-GUILHEM-LE-DÉSERT (90m)	4.6	32.9	2.8	20.4
SAINT-JEAN-DE-FOS (100m) [640.5/77.5]	4.6	**37.5**	2.9	**23.3**

See map and profile at the beginning of Stage 14.

An early start from La Vacquerie is recommended to avoid the heat exhaustion that could well occur in the middle of a very hot day on the exceedingly steep ascent towards Saint-Baudille mountain. The ascent is so steep in places that most will be pushing their bikes up these sections, with plenty of rests between short strenuous pushes! But once the main climb is over, the terrain, although rarely very easy, is not especially difficult for most of the rest of the way.

The trail climbs up to just below the summit of Saint-Baudille, easily recognised from afar by its tall aerial. There follows an excellent ridge heading northeast and offering superb views of these limestone mountains. After crossing the D122 the route turns to head south, mainly on good tracks and forest roads.

Take advantage of every patch of tree shade you can find before another steep climb (but fear not – it is not in the same category as the earlier Saint-Baudille ascent!) up to the col below the summit of Max Nègre. From there it is a long, long descent out of the mountains, passing the Maison Forestière des Plos, where if you are lucky, you may be able to enjoy a cool refreshing drink, before arriving in the main square of Saint-Jean-de-Fos.

After refreshment, and perhaps finding accommodation for the night, take the detour of a few kilometres to visit the village of Saint-Guilhem-le-Désert, which lies on the pilgrim route to Santiago de Compostela, and wander along its narrow medieval streets and visit its church.

Facilities

Two *gîtes d'étape* are located between La Vacquerie and Saint-Jean-de-Fos, but both are somewhat off-route – the *gîte d'étape* Font du Griffe, south and beneath the mighty mountain of Saint-Baudille, and the *gîte d'étape* at Les Lavagnes. On the descent from the Max Nègre col the route passes by the Maison Forestière des Plos, another *gîte d'étape*, but only open during the main season.

This stage ends at Saint-Jean-de-Fos, where there are two restaurant–cafés, an épicerie, boulangerie and a *gîte d'étape/chambres d'hôtes* (Au Pays des Orjouliers). Some, however, may wish to spend the night in the very attractive, but touristy village of Saint-Guilhem-le-Désert, where there is both *gîte d'étape* and hotel accommodation. The usual restaurants, cafés and tourist shops will also be found here.

Places of Interest
Saint-Jean-de-Fos
Famed in earlier centuries for its potters and their wares, Saint-Jean-de-Fos is now much better known for its vineyards and wineries.

Pont du Diable
This photogenic 11th-century bridge spans the deep l'Hérault Gorge, just outside Saint-Jean-de-Fos. Today the 'Devil's Bridge' sits alone in retirement, modern traffic crossing the river a few hundred metres downstream, over a modern road bridge that carries the D4.

Cathedral, Saint-Guilhem-le-Désert

Saint-Guilhem-le-Désert

Guillaume d'Orange, cousin of Charlemagne, founded a monastery here in the early ninth century. After Guillaume's death in AD812, his reputation and relics attracted large numbers of pilgrims, and the village of Saint-Guilhem-le-Désert grew up around the monastery to provide for these travellers. During the Middle Ages it became an important staging post on the pilgrim route to Compostela in Spain. Today its narrow streets, historic buildings and abbey church continue to attract many visitors.

GTMC MOUNTAIN BIKE TRAIL

The GTMC stage over the hills between Col du Vent and Saint-Jean-de-Fos is a tough one, particularly the extremely steep ascent to Saint-Baudille mountain. Those wishing to avoid this stretch can take the much easier and quicker road bike alternative via Arboras, described below.

Return on the D9 to the Col du Vent. The GTMC turns left onto a track heading southeast towards the peak of Saint-Baudille. Cross a surfaced lane after almost a kilometre and continue ahead on the main track. The climb becomes ever steeper, and most will have to resort to pushing their bike. At a junction be sure to take a left turn, as the variant route to the right is very technical and dangerous.

Climb very steeply, taking zigzags wherever possible, to reach a wide dirt road (the aerial access road). Follow this uphill for 200 metres. Turn left at the top of the hill on the left of the giant aerial, to pass a barrier and follow the track heading northeast along the ridge. The track continues for about 5km until turning to the south and descending to the D122.

Turn left along this road for overnight accommodation in the hamlet of Les Lavagnes, otherwise cross the D122 and take the track ahead. Keep to this main track, following the green GT de l'Hérault marker posts, eventually climbing to pass a large tank on the left (no. 152) and reaching a barrier over the track.

Climb ahead, southeast, on the main track to head towards the col to the south of the peak of Max Nègre. Then begin the long descent from the col towards Saint-Jean-de-Fos. After about 2.5km you will pass on your left the Maison Forestière des Plos, a *gîte d'étape*, which also sells drinks to visitors in the main season. Concentration and care is required on this very long descent. Eventually the trail passes through vineyards to reach a junction – here turn left on a narrow lane heading east towards the D141 in Saint-Jean-de-Fos.

Saint-Jean-de-Fos marks the end of this stage, but a visit to the picturesque and historic village of Saint-Guilhem-le-Desèrt, with its famous abbey, is highly recommended, an easy and pleasant cycle ride from Saint-Jean. To reach Saint-Guilhem-le-Desèrt, first descend northeast out of Saint-Jean-de-Fos to the Pont

Climbing to the col of Max Nègre

du Diable. Here turn left along the D4, cycling up the Hérault valley for just over 3km to the access road to Saint-Guilhem.

ROAD BIKE ALTERNATIVE

See 'Stage Maps for the Road Bike Alternative', after the end of Stage 17.
An excellent stage in superb countryside, but another hilly route. Head south from La Vacquerie on the D9 via the Col du Vent to Arboras. Continue southeast to La Meillade and Montpeyroux, taking the D141 to Saint-Jean-de-Fos. 22km from La Vacquerie to Saint-Jean-de-Fos. The easy detour to Saint-Guilhem-le-Désert (see above) is then highly recommended.

WALKING TRAIL – 1 DAY

A long day's walking, with considerable ascent and much more descent as the trail climbs over the last mountain obstacle before the coastal plain. The terrain is nevertheless relatively easy for a walker – mainly on good tracks, and the walker who has got this far should be trail fit by now!

Vineyards on approach to Saint-Jean-de-Fos

There are several possibilities for shortening the day.

Firstly, the initial 3.8km can be avoided by taking a taxi from La Vacquerie to the Col du Vent.

Secondly, there is a trail from Saint-Baudille that descends directly to La Font du Griffe on the south side of the mountain, where there is the possibility of *gîte d'étape* accommodation. This option cuts the route down by about 8km, to a much more manageable length. (This is the variant *not* recommended to mountain bikers unless they are very experienced and technically competent, but it should present no untoward difficulties for the walker.)

Thirdly, there is the possibility of overnight accommodation in a gîte in the hamlet of Les Lavagnes, less than a kilometre off-route on the D122.

Finally, the IGN map shows a trail descending from Max Nègre (Roc de la Bissonne) directly to Saint-Guilhem-le-Désert, where there is both hotel and *gîte d'étape* accommodation (but note that the author has reconnoitred neither the GTMC variant, nor the Max Nègre to Saint-Guilhem-le-Désert path).

STAGE 16

Saint-Jean-de-Fos to Montpellier

	Distance	39.5km (24.5 miles)	Ascent	266m (873ft)
	Off-road	39%	Descent	400m (1312ft)

Location	Distance (km)		Distance (miles)	
	Sectional	Cumulative	Sectional	Cumulative
SAINT-JEAN-DE-FOS (100m)				
Aniane	4.8	4.8	3.0	3.0
La Boissière	7.3	12.1	4.5	7.5
MONTARNAUD (110m)	5.8	17.9	3.6	11.1
LA PAILLADE (80m)	12.6	30.5	7.8	18.9
MONTPELLIER (30m) [680/38]	9.0	**39.5**	5.6	**24.5**

If you follow the official route of the GTMC today, mountain biking difficulties are not all behind you because you are out of the mountains and on the coastal plain – there are still some steep sections over very difficult terrain. However these can easily be avoided, if you've had enough rough stuff for one trip, by keeping to the roads (see Road Bike Alternative, below).

The GTMC follows a GR route for most of this stage, linking a number of villages and small towns of varying sizes as we head ever closer to the outskirts of Montpellier. Riding difficulties remain to the bitter end, until a succession of small bridges has been negotiated with care, and you enter an urban park in the Montpellier suburb of La Paillade. From here you can either cycle into the city centre, or take your bike into Montpellier on one of the city trams. La Paillade marks the end of GTMC waymarking – you will see no more

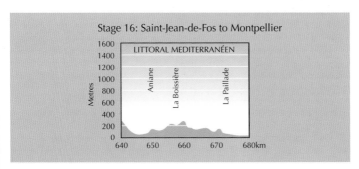

Stage 16: Saint-Jean-de-Fos to Montpellier

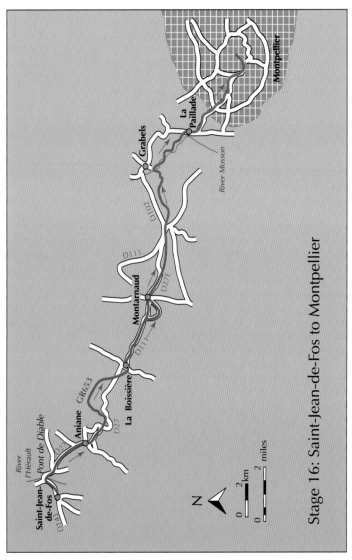

Stage 16: Saint-Jean-de-Fos to Montpellier

waymarks for the route from here all the way to the end of the trail at Sète. It would certainly be possible for strong riders to continue all the way to Sète in one day, but the route has been split into two stages in this book to allow plenty of time to enjoy the elegant city of Montpellier, with its many historic buildings and museums, leaving your last ride and celebrations for the following day.

Facilities
Montarnaud, at approximately the halfway point of the stage, is a good place for a relaxing stop, enjoying one of the excellent cakes from its *patisserie* or coffee in the village café opposite.

Montpellier, the largest city on the route since Clermont-Ferrand at the beginning of this adventure, has all the facilities you would expect, including hotels and restaurants of all grades, an 89-place youth hostel, a large tourist office and a mainline railway station.

Places of Interest
Aniane
The site of an eighth-century Benedictine abbey, now destroyed, this sizeable town is today a centre for viticulture.

Montpellier
A day can easily be spent in this elegant university city. The large central open square, the Place de la Comédie, is lined with many restaurants and cafés and has a bustling nightlife. The wide boulevards are lined with many large 17th- and 18th-century buildings, some of which house the city's numerous museums, the most important of which is the Musée Fabre. When tired of the latter, head through Montpellier's own *arc de triomphe* to stroll in the smart formal gardens of the Promenade du Peyrou. The view of the city from the top of the cathedral bell tower is stunning.

GTMC MOUNTAIN BIKE TRAIL
From Saint-Jean-de-Fos descend to the River Hérault at the Pont de Diable, and from here turn right onto the D27. After about 400 metres the GT34 leaves our trail by heading left on the D27. The GTMC continues southeast on the D27 for a further 3km to the small town of Aniane. From here onwards the GTMC follows the line of the GR653 all the way to La Paillade on the outskirts of Montpellier, so the way-marking you now follow is the red/white paint flashes of this long-distance trail.

Leave Aniane on the D27 signposted to La Boissière. About 250 metres after the sign indicating the limit of Aniane, turn right off the D27 and follow red/white

Le Pont du Diable (Alan Sides)

waymarks for about 250 metres to cross the main road again and then climb on a stony track. Near the top bear right (red/white waymark) and descend to reach and turn left on a smooth track.

At a junction turn right to pass under a bridge. Follow this disused railway line, passing a small tarn on your right, to reach and cross the D27 again. Take the track opposite, by a metal cross. Within 150 metres this track becomes surfaced. Follow red/white waymarks into the village of La Boissière.

Locate the D111 on the outskirts of La Boissière and follow it, direction Montarnaud, for almost 2km. Here leave it on the left for a track (red/white waymarks) into the woods, which soon returns to the D111. Cycle southeast along this road until, 3km from La Boissière, a large cross on a tall pedestal is reached – this is the Croix de Félix.

The actual line of the GTMC follows the GR653 eastwards down to Montarnaud. However, this descent is extremely difficult and dangerous with a bike, so it is strongly recommended that you remain on the D111 all the way to Montarnaud.

Exit Montarnaud on the D27E, and after about 1.2km bear right onto an old road, which runs parallel and south of the D27E. Bear to the left at a junction and continue until you reach the D111 road. Turn right for a few hundred metres, and then at the junction with the D102 look for and follow a track that heads eastwards, passing to the south of a go-carting circuit. Continue across this plateau, eventually descending very steeply on a narrow path (take great care).

After the descent on the outskirts of Grabels the trail heads southeastwards, crossing the Mosson river and then following its line, re-crossing it twice more. The second bridge is narrow and difficult to cross with a bike, so care is required. The trail emerges into an urban park in La Paillade. At this point the mountain biking trail has finally come to an end, as from here to Sète there are no particular difficulties, apart from sometimes coping with heavy traffic.

Heavy traffic is never more of a problem than in the following section into the centre of Montpellier – the wise will take an urban tram into the centre of town, and bicycles are carried free of charge.

If you do decide to cycle into Montpellier, follow cycle route No. 10 from La Paillade to the *arc de triomphe*. Alternatively, first follow the wide Avenue de l'Europe southwards, turn left into the Rue du Professeur-Blayac. At the large Alco roundabout take the second exit, the Rue d'Alco. Follow this to enter the Avenue de Lodève. Later bear left into the Rue du Faubourg du Courreau. On entering the historic centre, keep ahead along the Rue Saint-Guilhem to reach the heart of the city.

Arc de triomphe, Montpellier (Alan Sides)

Real and painted people, Montpellier (Alan Sides)

ROAD BIKE ALTERNATIVE

See 'Stage Maps for the Road Bike Alternative', after the end of Stage 17.
There is a direct and pleasant road route from Saint-Jean-de-Fos all the way to La Paillade on the outskirts of Montpellier, although traffic will increase as you get closer to Montpellier. The D27 leads southeast from Saint-Jean-de-Fos to Aniane and on to La Boissière. From here the D111 leads to Montarnaud. Continue in the same direction on the D27 to Bel-Air, and then the D102 to Grabels, from where the D127 leads to La Paillade. 34km from Saint-Jean-de-Fos to La Paillade.

WALKING TRAIL – 1 TO 2 DAYS

A relatively easy walk, but a long one to complete in a day. There is limited opportunity for overnight accommodation in the villages passed en route, but if you can manage the 30.5km to the outskirts of Montpellier at La Paillade, then a tram or bus will whisk you quickly to the centre of the city. Those intent on walking every step of the way can easily return to La Paillade by public transport on the following day. Do consider the idea of urban walking – Montpellier is a vibrant city, full of interest, even in the outer suburbs, although care is needed crossing the often busy roads.

It may also be possible to take a bus from Montarnaud into Montpellier and back the next morning, so splitting the stage into two roughly equal and very manageable walking sections.

There is little opportunity to avoid a road walk from Saint-Jean-de-Fos to Aniane, but once there the GTMC follows the GR653 all the way to La Paillade, an under-used long-distance path that has considerable variety and makes, quite frankly, a better walking route than a biking trail!

STAGE 17

Montpellier to Sète

| Distance | 38.0km (23.6 miles) | Ascent | 0m (0ft) |
| Off-road | 63% | Descent | 0m (0ft) |

Location	Distance (km)		Distance (miles)	
	Sectional	*Cumulative*	*Sectional*	*Cumulative*
MONTPELLIER (30m)				
Mas des Salins	9.0	9.0	5.6	5.6
Palavas-les-Flots (Étang du Méjean)	2.0	11.0	1.2	6.8
Maguelone	4.3	15.3	2.7	9.5
Étang d'Ingril	8.9	24.2	5.5	15.0
SÈTE (highest point 121m) [718/0]	13.8	**38.0**	8.6	**23.6**

Although a metropolis bustling with traffic, Montpellier is nevertheless a cycle-friendly city, with an abundance of cycle paths. It is a good idea to pick up a free map of the city at the large *office de tourism* in the Place de la Comédie, in the centre of the city, before setting out on this last stage of the journey, as a city map will help you to follow accurately the route out to the canal.

This last stage of the GTMC is really a coda to the whole route – it is quite unlike the remainder of the trail, the Massif Central now having been left well behind and replaced by the Mediterranean coast. There are no difficulties on this stage, but do be aware that the route from the Mas des Salins along the canal system towards Sète is closed in periods of heavy rain and flood.

Once you reach the Canal du Rhône the cycling is very relaxed for mile after mile, on good, firm sandy tracks, with the blue Mediterranean over to

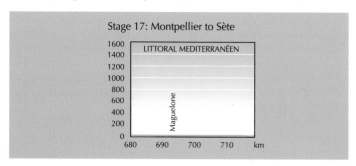

Stage 17: Montpellier to Sète

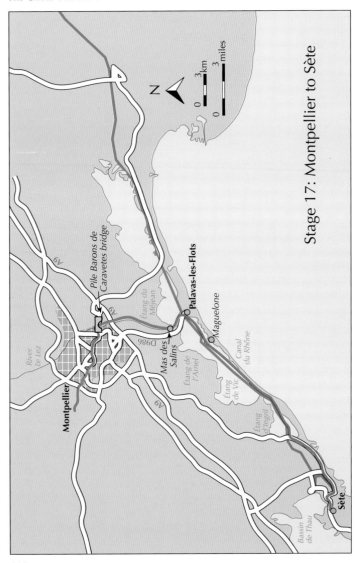

Stage 17: Montpellier to Sète

Preparing for the joust, Sète

your left, and the canal and a succession of artificial lakes, or *étangs*, on your right. You will no doubt meet many other cyclists and walkers out enjoying the trail, particularly at weekends or during the main summer holiday season. (Do not forget sunscreen and sunhat, as there is virtually no possibility of finding shade.)

After the slow progress made over much of the GTMC, you will be amazed at the speed at which you effortlessly ride along these flat, smooth cycleways! It is no more than a half-day ride from Montpellier to Sète, so there is plenty of time to explore this 'island' peninsula town, and celebrate your completion of the Grand Traverse of the Massif Central, from central France's main city to the Mediterranean sea.

Facilities

Those looking for a seaside campsite will find one at Palavas-les-Flots. Sète has all the shops, cafés and restaurants you could possibly want, so select a good one for a celebratory meal. The town has many hotels and, like Montpellier, a large youth hostel. Frequent trains operate from Sète railway station to Montpellier to the northeast, and on to Nîmes (for connections back to Clermont-Ferrand) or to Narbonne, Béziers and Carcassonne in the southwest.

Places of Interest
Canal du Rhône

From the River Rhône at Tarascon, the canal runs southwestwards through the Camargue, after which it passes south of Montpellier to the enormous Bassin de Thau, alongside Sète. From there it continues to meet the famed Canal du Midi, east of Béziers. Many pink flamingos will be seen on the numerous lakes (étangs) alongside this canal, which is passed on the way from Palavas-les-Flots to Sète.

Maguelone: Island and Cathedral

The short detour from the Canal du Rhône across a causeway to the 'island within a lake' that is Maguelone is highly recommended, to visit the tranquil 11th-century cathedral, which has recently undergone a superb restoration.

Sète

An important Mediterranean port for over 300 years, it is the upper parts of Sète, built on the slopes of Mont St-Clair, that are the most interesting. The adjacent Bassin de Thau produces abundant mussels and oysters, which are sold in local markets and restaurants. If you are fortunate enough to arrive on a summer's day when the *joutes nautiques* contests are being staged, you will enjoy a unique centuries-old pageant. This light-hearted water-jousting contest consists of teams of young men in boats attempting to knock their rivals into the water using long jousting lances.

Birds flying towards Maguelone

Looking down on Sète (Alan Sides)

GTMC MOUNTAIN BIKE TRAIL

From the *office de tourism* in the Place de la Comédie, head southeast along the Rue de Verdun, taking the second road on the left, the Rue Ollivier. Cross the Avenue Henri Frenay and continue along the Avenue du Pont Juvénal. Cross the Avenue des États du Languedoc, still on the Avenue du Pont Juvénal. At the Place Faulquier take the Chemin des Barques, which ends at the Place Jean Bene. Here cross the river, Le Lez, over the Pile Barons de Caravetes.

On the opposite bank turn right to cycle south alongside the river on the Allée du Capitaine Dreyfus, leaving Montpellier. Keep by the eastern bank of the river, passing to the west of the suburb of Lattes. The suburbs have faded by the time you reach the Mas des Salins, on the Étang du Méjean, about 7km after the Pile Barons de Caravetes bridge.

Cross the causeway between the Étang du Méjean and the Étang de l'Arnel to pass Premières Cabanes, and arrive at the junction of four canals (Les Quatre Canaux) on the outskirts of Palavas-les-Flots. Turn right here, passing under the Palavas bridge, and continue along the Canal du Rhône, between the Étang de l'Arnel on your right and the Étang du Prévost and the Mediterranean on your left.

After 3.3km turn left to take the track to Maguelone, to visit the cathedral of Maguelone, situated on its own small island between the Étang du Prévost to the northeast and the Étang de Pierre Blanche to the southwest.

Return to the canal track and continue southwestwards for many more kilometres. The track passes alongside the Étang de Vic and then the Étang d'Ingril. A kilometre after passing under the road bridge south of Frontignan, you will reach and cross the last bridge over the canal.

From here take to the road system for the last 5km to Sète, taking especial care, as this area is often busy with both local and tourist traffic. Once you have reached the rock cone of Sète, head uphill to the *table d'orientation* at its highest point, to admire the panoramic view before descending back to the town for a celebratory meal.

ROAD BIKE ALTERNATIVE

See the map for Stage 17 GTMC Mountain Bike Trail.
All but the most frail of road bikes will cope with the terrain on the GTMC between Montpellier and Sète, and this route, very popular with cyclists of every ability and type of bike, is highly recommended. The alternative on the often busy roads is not worth the mention.

WALKING TRAIL – 1 TO 2 DAYS

There is no better trail than that of the GTMC from Montpellier to Sète, popular with both walkers and cyclists. Although a long distance to walk in one day, the terrain is flat and easy going, and should present few problems – other than possible over-exposure to the sun – to walkers who have travelled al the way from Clermont-Ferrand on foot. It is easy enough to split into two days if required, however, as public transport to either Montpellier or Sète for accommodation is plentiful in this populated area.

STAGE MAPS FOR
THE ROAD BIKE ALTERNATIVE

These sketch maps provide an overview of the road bike alternative route to the GTMC. Less confident or skilled mountain bikers may wish to follow some of these alternatives to avoid more difficult sections of the trail, particularly during bad weather or after heavy rain, when some of the unsurfaced tracks can become quagmires.

The whole of Stage 17 of the GTMC is suitable for road cyclists, so there is no separate road bike description or map for this stage.

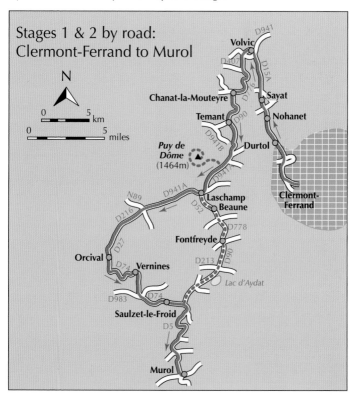

Stages 1 & 2 by road:
Clermont-Ferrand to Murol

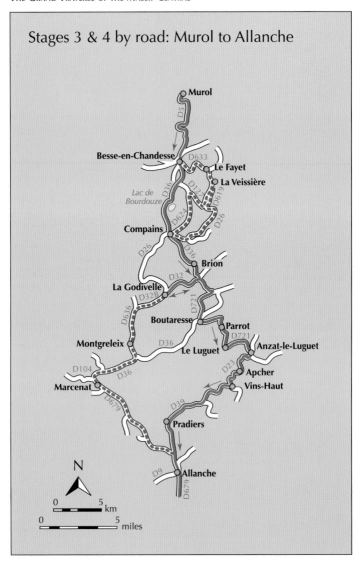

Stages 3 & 4 by road: Murol to Allanche

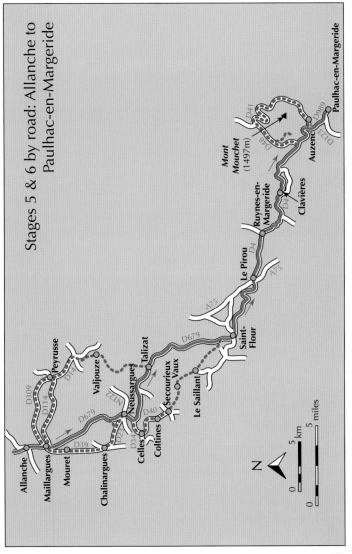

Stages 5 & 6 by road: Allanche to Paulhac-en-Margeride

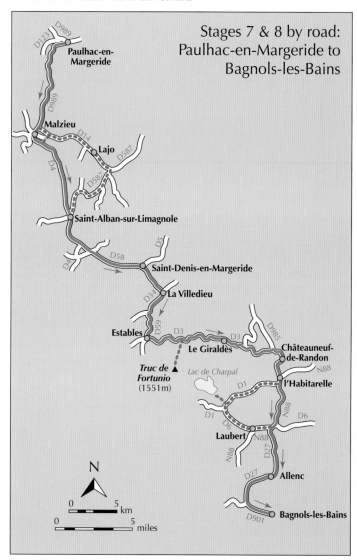

Stages 7 & 8 by road:
Paulhac-en-Margeride to
Bagnols-les-Bains

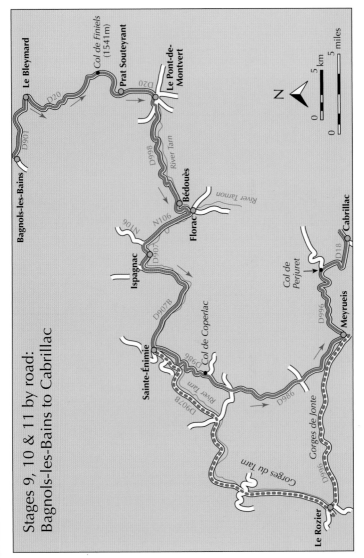

Stages 9, 10 & 11 by road:
Bagnols-les-Bains to Cabrillac

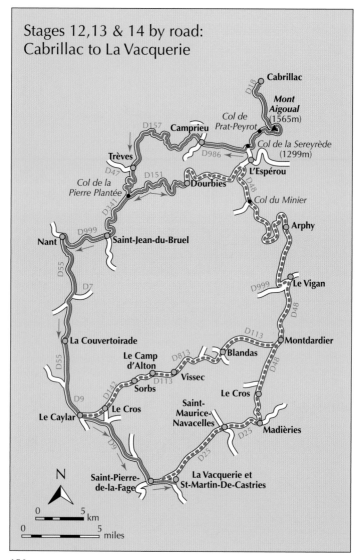

Stages 12, 13 & 14 by road: Cabrillac to La Vacquerie

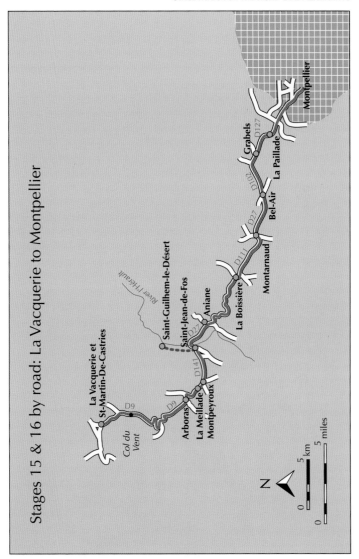

Stages 15 & 16 by road: La Vacquerie to Montpellier

Walking the bike through Saint-Guilhem-le-Désert (Stage 15, photo: Alan Sides)

APPENDIX A

Budget Accommodation along the GTMC

If you are calling France from the UK, dial 00 33 and omit the first zero in the phone numbers shown below.

Locations listed in brackets, for example (MONTLOSIER), are off-route.

CLERMONT-FERRAND
Youth Hostel, Auberge de Jeunesse
FUAJ
Tel 04.73.92.26.39.

Éthic Étape Home Dôme.
Tel 04.73.29.46.67
www.ethic-etapes.fr
E.home.dome@wanadoo.fr

LASCHAMP
Espace Volcan *gîte d'étape*/ hotel-restaurant complex
Tel 04.73.62.26.00
www.espace.volcan.fr
espace.volcan@wanadoo.fr

Gîte-Auberge Archipel Volcans
Tel 04.73.62.15.15
www.archipel-volcans.com
info@archipel-volcans.com

(MONTLOSIER)
Gîte d'étape du PNR des Volcans d'Auvergne
Tel 04.73.65.64.00 or 04.73.65.64.21
Open from the beginning of May to the end of October; to reserve an evening meal tel 04.73.65.69.95

ORCIVAL – SERVIÈRES
Gîte d'étape du Café du Lac, 4km from Orcival by the Lac de Servières
Tel 04.73.65.93.63

PESSADE
Gîte d'étape de Pessade
Tel 04.73.79.31.07;
to reserve an evening meal
tel 04.73.65.69.95

CHAUMIANE
Gîte d'étape
Tel 04.73.71.21.05

LA GODIVELLE
Gîte d'étape des Sagnes
Tel 04.73.71.92.60
contact@gitesdessagnes.com

CHALINARGUES
Gîte d'étape communal
Tel 04.71.20.03.52 or 04.71.20.07.60
(mairie)

PAULHAC-EN-MARGERIDE
Gîte d'étape
Tel 04.66.31.73.46

LE SAUVAGE
Gîte d'étape
Tel 04.71.74.40.30

LA BARAQUE-DES-BOUVIERS
Gîte d'étape
Tel 04.66.47.41.54 or 04.66.48.48.48

LE GIRALDÈS
Gîte d'étape
Tel 04.66.47.92.70

LAUBERT
Gîte d'étape (Centre d'Accueil)
Tel 04.66.47.73.08

(STATION LE MONT LOZÈRE)
Gîte d'étape Le Refuge
Tel 04.66.48.62.83

LE PONT-DE-MONTVERT
Gîte d'étape communal in the
Ecomuseum building
Contact the mairie, tel 04.66.45.80.10

(MIJAVOLS)
Gîte d'étape, 5km off-route between Le
Pont-de-Montvert and Florac in the area
of the Signal du Bougès
Tel 04.66.45.09.04

FLORAC
(i) *Gîte d'étape* La Carline,
18 Rue du Pêcher
Tel 04.66.45.24.54
**www.causses-cevennes.com/
lagrave.htm**
lagrave.alain@wanadoo.fr
(ii) *Gîte d'étape* communal
Tel 04.66.45.23.98 or
06.79.95.67.12

(MEYRUEIS)
Gîte d'étape La Draille, no kitchen
Tel 04.66.45.65.37

(MARJOAB)
Gîte d'étape, 2.5km southwest of
Meyrueis, 13.5km off-route GTMC;
open April to August
Tel 04.66.45.64.18 or
04.66.45.53.59

LE ROZIER
Gîte d'étape Gévaudan
Tel 05.65.62.62.70

PEYRELEAU
Gîte Évolutions les Corniches de la
Jonte
Tel 05.65.62.60.93 or 06.81.76.68.54

CABRILLAC
Gîte d'étape, Refuge des Drailles; open
July and August, and abri (without
guardian) April to June and September
to November
Tel 04.66.45.62.21 or 04.66.81.62.64
or 04.66.83.38.34

(AIRE DE CÔTE)
Gîte d'étape, 11km from Cabrillac and
7km from Mont Aigoual
Tel 04.66.44.70.47

MONT AIGOUAL
Refuge Mont Aigoual
Tel 04.67.82.62.78 or 04.67.82.25.10

(CAMPRIEU)
Gîte d'étape Au Bord du Lac, in Le
Devois, 1km east of Camprieu, on the
shore of a small lake; only open in July
and August; no kitchen
Tel 04.67.82.61.20

DOURBIES
Gîte d'étape communal; enquire at the nearby village shop/café/restaurant in the village centre
Tel 04.67.81.49.74

Maison de vacances; no kitchen facilities, but meals provided
Tel 04.67.82.74.85

(ALZON)
Gîte d'étape et de séjour Le Colombier
Tel 04.67.81.08.99

LA COUVERTOIRADE
Gîte d'étape Gîte de la Cité
Tel 05.65.58.17.75 or 06.03.08.13.98

LA VACQUERIE
Gîte d'étape du Club Alpin Français (CAF)
Tel 04.67.95.16.88

Gîte d'étape et de séjour Pouss'Combe
Tel 04.67.44.68.99

(FONT DU GRIFFE)
Gîte d'étape, below and south of Saint-Baudille
Tel 04.67.88.60.59

(LES LAVAGNES)
Gîte du Mas Aubert
Tel 04.67.73.10.25

SAINT-JEAN-DE-FOS
Gîte d'étape Au Pays des Orjouliers; private rooms, but no evening meal provided
Tel 04.67.57.36.00.

SAINT-GUILHEM-LE-DÉSERT
Refuge du Club Alpin Français (CAF)
Tel 04.67.57.48.63 or 06.60.57.07.51

Gîte d'étape de la Tour
Tel 04.67.57.34.00

Gîte d'étape Le Logis des Penitents
Tel 04.67.57.48.63 or 06.60.57.07.51

MONTPELLIER
Youth Hostel, Auberge de Jeunesse FUAJ, In the Rue des Écoles, 1km from the railway station
Tel 04.67.60.32.22

SÈTE
Youth Hostel, Auberge de Jeunesse FUAJ, In the Rue du Général-Revest
Tel 04.67.53.46.68

There are several other *gîtes d'étape* in the Auvergne, Chaîne des Puys, Parc Naturel Régional des Volcans d'Auvergne, Cézallier, Cantal, Margeride, Cévennes, Causses and Mediterranean regions. Contact details of the *gîtes d'étape* in the area will be found at www.gites-refuges.com.

For information on the many hotels, *chambres d'hôtes* and camping sites along the GTMC, contact the various local tourist offices (see Appendix 4 for contact details of some of the main tourist offices in the area). The Parc National des Cévennes (see Appendix 4) provides a free leaflet entitled 'Les *Gîtes d'étape* en Cévennes', which is regularly updated.

APPENDIX B

Other Long Distance Trails along the GTMC

The Massif Central has a greater concentration and mileage of long-distance GR trails than any other region of France, a testament to the high quality of walking and off-road cycling to be enjoyed there. Details of the main trails in the region are summarised below. Many of them are encountered on the GTMC, either because they are crossed over, or, in many cases, because they are followed for varying distances, sometimes many miles. Mountain bikes are allowed along several sections of these GR and other routes, but if permissible access, or the suitability of riding on a particular trail, are in doubt, always revert to the nearby minor road network. Generally, when a trail is called a chemin (track) it is usually, but not always, permissible to take a mountain bike along it, but this is less often the case with a sentier (footpath). You must comply with any signs forbidding the use of a bicycle on a trail.

Some of the trails included below are described in detail in Cicerone guidebooks in English (eg the GR4, GR40, GR68 and GR70), and the others are covered by Topo Guides, in French, published by the Fédération Française de la Randonnée Pédestre. All these guidebooks can be ordered from outlets in the UK, for example Stanfords, the Map Shop, or over

the web from Au Vieux Campeur, a huge outdoor store based in Paris (see Appendix D). They are also available from book shops locally in the Massif Central.

GR30 – Tour des Lacs d'Auvergne

170km (106 miles). A circular route based on the Monts-Dore, and visiting the principal crater and glacial lakes in the area. The trail meets the GTMC at Orcival and at Murol (Stage 2).

GR33

A linear west-to-east route from la Combraille to the Monts du Forez, passing through the Chaîne des Puys south of the Puy de Dôme, where it encounters the GTMC (Stage 1).

GR4 – Sentier Méditerranée – Océan

A very long west-to-east route from Royan on the Atlantic coast to Grasse above the Côte d'Azur. The route passes through the following regions: Océan, Saintonge, Limousin, Auvergne, Margeride, Cévennes, Vallée du Rhone, Gorges du Verdon and Provence. It crosses the RLS Trail at Langogne. Two Cicerone guidebooks, both by Alan Castle, cover the most spectacular sections of the GR4, in the Auvergne (Volvic to Langogne) and in Provence (Grasse to Langogne). See Appendix C, Further Reading.

The GR4 and the GTMC are in close proximity in the Chaîne des Puys volcanic region of the Auvergne and in the Margeride. Much of the GTMC from Volvic to Laschamp follows the GR4 (Stage 1), and the trail again is encountered at Saint Flour.

GR40 – Tour du Velay

100 miles (161km) encircling Le Puy-en-Velay. The itinerary includes Vorey, Mont-Bar, Allègre, Siaugues, St-Remain, La Durande, Montbonnet, Le Bouchet St-Nicolas, Goudet, Alleyrac, Les Estables, Mont Mézenc, Saint Front, Boussoulet, Mont Meygal, Le Pertuis and St-Julien du Pinet. This area is to the east of the GTMC. It is encountered several times on the RLS Trail in the Velay. There is a Cicerone guidebook to the Tour of the Velay, also by the author (see Appendix C).

GR41

The trail passes through the central Auvergne from Brioude to La Bourboule and Super Besse, and on to Evaux-les-Baines (235km/146 miles). It continues to Cher, Creuse and the Allier valley, a region to the east of the GTMC.

GR43 – La Draille de la Margeride (Tour de la Margeride)

An 88km (55 mile) route following an ancient drove road linking the GR4 at Sainte-Eulalie to the GR7 at the Col des Faïsses, west of Barre des Cévennes. It is a harsh trail, passing through uninhabited country with little opportunity, with the exception of Florac, of finding accommodation. The route encounters the GTMC in the Margeride and at Florac.

GR44

An 87km (54 mile) spur of the GR4 running west from Les Vans on the GR4 to Villefort, Mas d'Orcières, Col de la Loubière and Champerboux. The route passes just to the south of Le Bleymard, where it encounters the GTMC (Stage 9) and crosses the Robert Louis Stevenson Trail.

GR400 – Tour des Volcans du Cantal

Plenty of ascent and descent on this circular trail of the Cantal, an area just to the west of the GTMC (Stages 3 and 4). 146km (91 miles) in length, the tour visits most of the principal peaks and valleys in the region.

GR441 – Tour de la Chaîne des Puys, Volcans d'Auvergne

An elongated, circular route 108km (67 miles) in length, to the west of Clermont-Ferrand in the Département of the Puy de Dôme. The GTMC closely follows the route of the GR441 from Volvic to Le Variant and from Puy Chopine to a little after Laschamp, and then from Orcival to Pessade (Stages 1 and 2).

GR60

This linear trail leaves the GR6 south-east of Aubrac and heads southeast to Auxillac. From there it continues in a southeasterly direction to Sainte-Énimie, and then across the Causses to the Col de Perjuret and on to the summit of Mont Aigoual. The GTMC encounters the GR60 at Sainte-Énimie and follows it between Nivoliers and the Col de Perjuret (Stage 11).

GR65 – Chemin de Saint Jacques de Compostelle (Way of St James)

A modern route following the line of the medieval trail of pilgrimage to Santiago de Compostela in northwest Spain. The trail of some 800km (500 miles) to the Spanish border starts at Le Puy-en-Velay and heads southwest to cross the Pyrenees near the town of St-Jean-Pied-de-Port. Bikers and walkers on the GTMC will probably meet many pilgrims on the Way of St James when the two trails meet at Le Sauvage (Stage 7) There are Cicerone cycling and walking guides to this famous route (see Appendix C).

GR653

A variant of the Chemin de Saint Jacques de Compostelle, which is followed by the GTMC from Saint-Jean-de-Fos to La Paillade on the outskirts of Montpellier (Stage 16).

GR66 – Tour du Mont Aigoual

A circuit of the southern part of the Cévennes from Dourbies via the Col des Portes, l'Espérou, Mont Aigoual, Aire de Côte, Cabrillac and Meyrueis. The 80km (50 mile) trail is encountered on the GTMC at Cabrillac and Mont Aigoual (Stage 12).

GR67 – Tour des Cévennes (Tour en Pays Cévenol)

A 130km (81 mile) trail encircling the valleys of the numerous Gardon rivers. From Anduze the trail heads to St-Felix-de-Pallières and Colognac and over the Col de Asclié and the Col du Pas to Aire de Côte, east of Mont Aigoual. The path continues to L'Hospitalet, Barre des Cévennes, Plan de Fontmort, Col de Jalcreste, and then south to St-André-de-Lancize, Mialet, Mas Soubeyran and back to Anduze. It encounters the GTMC on Mont Aigoual (Stage 12).

GR68 – Tour du Mont Lozère

A circular trail of 110km (68 miles), encircling the mountain massif in the Cévennes. From Villefort on the Paris–Nîmes railway line, the route includes Cubières, Orcières, Col des Sagnoles, Florac, Croix de Berthel, L'Aubaret, Gourdouse and Les Bouzèdes. Much of this is within the Cévennes National Park. The GTMC encounters this trail at Auriac above Bagnols-les-Bains (Stage 9), and later follows a section of it on the route from the Col du Sapet to Florac (Stage 10).

GR7 – Sentier Vosges – Pyrénées

Another ultra-long-distance route, stretching from Ballon d'Alsace to Andorra in the Pyrenees. On the way the route passes through the Vosges, Plateau de Langres, Côte d'Or, Mâconnais, Beaujolais, Lyonnais, Vivarais, Cévennes, Haut Languedoc, Corbières and Pyrenees. It passes close to the GTMC in the Cévennes.

GR70 – the Robert Louis Stevenson Trail

This trail, now one of the most popular long-distance routes in France, follows closely, but not exactly, the route taken in 1878 by the celebrated 19th-century Scottish writer Robert Louis Stevenson, and described in his book Travels with a Donkey in the Cévennes. Starting at Le Monastier-sur-Gazeille near Le Puy-en-Velay, the trail traverses the Velay and Cévennes to St-Jean-du-Gard, a distance of 226km (140 miles). The RLS Trail follows a similar route to the section of the GTMC from Mont Lozère via Le Pont-de-Montvert to Florac (Stages 9 and 10). The GR430 links Le Puy with Le Monastier at the start of the trail and the GRs 61, 67 and 44D provide a trail from St-Jean-du-Gard to the large town of Alès (see Appendix C).

GR72

The GR72 links the GR4 near Le Bez to the GR7 at the Barre des Cévennes. The GTMC encounters this trail on the approach to Florac (Stage 10).

Tour de la Haute Auvergne

A GR de Pays, or regional trail, it covers an area to the southeast of Saint Flour by a series of loops visiting the Truyère gorges, Garabit Viaduct, Château d'Alleuze and the foothills of the Margeride. Unlike the standard GR trails this route is waymarked with red/yellow paint stripes.

GR de Pays Tour du Causse Méjean

This regional trail, 111km (69 miles) in length and waymarked with red/yellow paint stripes, encircles the high limestone Causse to the west of Florac, and is encountered on the GTMC at Mas-Saint-Chély (Stage 11).

E4

Sections of the GR7, GR72 and GR44 form part of the European Long Distance Path which runs from Rust in eastern Austria, across northern Switzerland and southern France to Fredes, southwest of Barcelona in Spain, a distance of 3414km (2122 miles). The E4 passes through the Cévennes National Park from Les Vans to Villefort and onto Mont Aigoual (Stage 12 of the GTMC) and then through the Haut-Languedoc Regional Park.

APPENDIX C
Further Reading

Grande Traversée du Massif Central à VTT. Des Volcans à la Méditerranée, Chamina 2002

The official French guidebook to the GTMC. The route is described and mapped on a series of 41 folded leaflets, which are housed in a folder. The publication also includes three introductory leaflets, a booklet offering practical advice on tackling the route and accommodation possibilities along the trail. This work is strongly recommended, even for those unable to read French, as it is the cheapest and most convenient way of acquiring all the IGN maps needed to follow the route (see Maps in the Introduction). Au Vieux Campeur in Paris (see Appendix D) usually stocks the publication, which can be ordered online.

Cycle Touring in France by Stephen Fox, Cicerone Press 2006

The book describes eight on-road cycle routes in various regions of the country. One of these is a 356km (221 mile) route crossing the Auvergne and Longuedoc from Meymac via Riom-ès-Montagnes, Saint Flour, Marvejols and Florac to Alès.

The Robert Louis Stevenson Trail – the GR70 from Le Puy to St-Jean-du-Gard by Alan Castle, Cicerone Press (2nd edition) 2007

The Chemin de Stevenson is one of France's most popular long-distance walks, traversing the Velay and the Cévennes from north to south, following a route similar to that taken by the 19th-century Scottish writer in 1878, as he researched his first successful book, Travels with a Donkey in the Cévennes. The route, which the author divides into 12 day-stages, easily fits into a fortnight's holiday. The RLS Trail follows a similar, but not identical route, to the section of the GTMC from Mont Lozère via Le Pont-de-Montvert to Florac (Stage 10).

Walks in Volcano Country by Alan Castle, Cicerone Press 1992

A guidebook describing two walks in the Auvergne. First, the Traverse of the High Auvergne (177km/110 miles or 257km/160 miles; 10 or 15 days), from Volvic across the Puy de Dome, Puy de Sancy and Cantal to Saint-Flour and on to Langogne, where it meets the RLS Trail. The first part of this trail, like the GTMC, crosses the Chaîne des Puys, Cantal and Margeride. It encounters the GTMC at Volvic, Laschamp and Saint Flour, before heading further east. Second, the Tour of the Velay, a 160km/100 mile (eight days) circular walk around Le Puy,

Entering Chalinargues

including Monts Mézenc and Meygal, a route which lies in the Auvergne to the east of the GTMC. Out-of-print at the time of writing, but a copy may be found in a local library, or from a second-hand book dealer.

The Way of St James: Le Puy to Santiago – A Cyclist's Guide by John Higginson, Cicerone Press 2005

The Way of St James: Le Puy to the Pyrenees by Alison Raju, Cicerone Press 2004

The latter is a walker's guide to the French section of the famous pilgrimage route. This popular trail to Santiago meets the GTMC between Chanaleilles and Le Sauvage (Stage 7).

Walking the French Gorges by Alan Castle, Cicerone Press 1993

This guidebook includes the GR4, a trail across the Cévennes from Les Vans, via Thines and Loubaresse, to Langogne, in an area to the east of the GTMC.

Walking in the Cévennes by Janette Norton, Cicerone Press 2002

31 day-walks in the region, plus a guide to the GR68, the Tour du Mont Lozère, the latter encountered on the GTMC.

Volcans et Lacs d'Auvergne, FFRP

Topo Guide (in French) to the GR4 in the Auvergne, the GR441 and the GR30. Describes the GR4 for 274km (170 miles) from Aubusson (west of Volvic) to Saint-Flour. Includes IGN maps with highlighted route.

Gorges de l'Ardèche à la Margeride, FFRP

A Topo Guide (in French). Describes the GR4 for 230km (143 miles) from Saint-Flour to Pont Saint-Esprit (on the Rhône). Also, the GR43 from Sainte-Eulalie via Florac to the Barre-des-Cévennes (88km/55 miles) and the GR44 from Vans to Champerboux (87km/54 miles). Includes IGN maps with highlighted routes.

Tours du Mont Lozère, FFRP

A Topo Guide (in French). Includes descriptions, with route highlighted on IGN maps, of the GR68 and the Tour du Causse Méjean. Sections of these trails provide alternative walking routes for a Grand Traverse of the Massif Central.

Tour du Mont Aigoual, FFRP

Topo Guide (in French) to the GR66, a circular 80km (50 mile) route via Dourbies, Meyrueis, Aire de Côte and Mont Aigoual. Includes IGN maps with highlighted route. A section of the GR6 is also included.

Cévennes, Montagne, Refuge, Terre de Rencontres by Alan Gas, Nouvelles Presses de Languedoc 2008

For those looking for a good coffee-table book as a momento of their journey, this is one of the best. Gas is a celebrated photographer and writer whose evocative photos capture the essence of this distinctive rural area.

General Tourist Guides

Both the Rough Guide and Lonely Planet series of guides to France are directed at the independent traveller, and compared to many other general tourist guidebooks, relatively light to carry. They include information on budget and other accommodation, including campsites. Michelin Green Guides to various regions of France are an alternative source of general tourist information (in French, but some volumes are available in English).

APPENDIX D
Useful Contacts

If you are calling France from the UK, dial 00 33 and omit the first zero in the French phone numbers shown below.

MAPS & GUIDEBOOKS

The Map Shop
15 High Street
Upton-upon-Severn
Worcestershire
WR8 OHJ
Freephone 0800 085 4080
www.themapshop.co.uk

Guidepost
Online service for maps and
guidebooks
www.guidepost.uk.com
mail@guidepost.uk.com

Stanfords
Maps and guidebooks
www.stanfords.co.uk

Au Vieux Campeur
48 Rue des Écoles
75005
Paris
France
www.auvieuxcampeur.fr
infos@auvieuxcampeur.fr

Nearest Metro station Maubert-Mutualité, and stores in several other French cities. Extensive range of French maps and guidebooks, which can be ordered online, paying by credit card.

IGN French mapping
www.ign.fr

Michelin French mapping
www.cartesetguides.michelin.fr

GITES AND REFUGES IN FRANCE
www.gites-refuges.com

Information on 4000 *gîtes d'étape* and refuges in France. You can use this useful website to find up-to-date details of the *gîtes d'étape* on the GTMC. There is an English language version and it is possible to search by long-distance trail, including the GTMC. Contact details for gîtes and refuges are given, and there are automatic links to some gîte websites, allowing online booking. The book *Gîtes d'étape de Randonnée et Refuges*, by Annick & Serge Mouraret, listing all of France's gîtes and refuges, can be purchased from this site.

TRANSPORT

French Railways (SNCF)
www.sncf.com
This is a French language website (with English language version available). For timetable enquiries and reservations: **www.voyages-sncf.com**

Eurostar
Timetables and bookings:
www.raileurope.co.uk or
www.eurostar.com

Seat 61
www.seat61.com
A very useful website that provides a great deal of information on rail travel throughout the world, including taking bicycles on European railways.

European Bike Express
3 Newfield Lane
South Cave
Hull
HU15 2JW
Tel 01430 422111, fax 01430 422877
www.bike-express.co.uk
info@bike-express.co.uk
Coach travel from Britain to France, with bike transport in custom-built trailers

WALKLING & CYCLING

GTMC
www.chamina.com
info@chamina.com

FFC (Fédération Française de Cyclisme)
www.ffc.fr

Cyclists Touring Club (CTC)
Parklands
Railton Road
Guildford
Surrey
GU2 9JX
Tel 0870 873 0061
www.ctc.org.uk
cycling@ctc.org.uk

Membership has various benefits for cyclists, including route and tour information, legal claims advice, cycle insurance and discounts with various suppliers.

FFRP (Fédération Française de la Randonnée Pédestre)
www.ffrandonnee.fr

An excellent site on all aspects of long-distance trails in France.

GENERAL TOURIST INFORMATION

Tourism in the Cévennes
www.cevennes-tourisme.fr

In French, but with English language option. Includes sections on where to stay, what to do, where to visit and where to walk.

Parc National des Cévennes
www.cevennes-parcnational.fr
info@cevennes-parcnational.fr

Largely French-language but some information is in English.

Département of Lozère and Cévennes
www.cevennes-lozere.com
Operated by the Pont-de-Montvert
tourist office,
tel 04.66.45.81.94.

Local Tourist Offices
The following websites are in French,
but those with English options are
asterisked (*)

Clermont-Ferrand:
www.clermont-fd.com (*)
tel 04.73.98.65.00

Volvic:
www.volvic-tourisme.com
tel 04.73.33.58.73

Saint-Flour:
www.saint-flour.com (*)
tel 04.71.60.22.50

Bagnols-les-Bains:
www.bagnols-les-bains.com
tel 04.66.47.61.13

Florac:
www.ville-florac.fr (*)
tel 04.66.45.01.14

Ispagnac:
www.ispagnac.com
tel 04.66.44.20.89

Sainte-Énimie:
www.gorgesdutarn.net tel
04.66.48.53.44

La Couvertoirade:
www.lacouvertoirade.com
tel 05.65.58.55.59

Saint-Guilhem-le-Désert:
www.saintguilhem-valleeherault.fr (*)
tel 04.67.57.44.33

Montpellier:
www.ot-montpellier.fr (*)
tel 04.67.60.60.60

Sète: **www.ot-sete.fr** (*)
tel 04.67.74.71.71

LISTING OF CICERONE GUIDES

Walking on the Brecon Beacons
Welsh Winter Climbs

AFRICA
Climbing in the Moroccan Anti-Atlas
Kilimanjaro – A Complete Trekker's
  Guide
Trekking in the Atlas Mountains

THE ALPS
100 Hut Walks in the Alps
Across the Eastern Alps: The E5
Alpine Points of View
Alpine Ski Mountaineering:
  Vol 1 – Western Alps
  Vol 2 – Central & Eastern Alps
Chamonix to Zermatt
Snowshoeing: Techniques and Routes
  in the Western Alps
Tour of Mont Blanc
Tour of Monte Rosa
Tour of the Matterhorn
Walking in the Alps

EASTERN EUROPE
High Tatras
Mountains of Romania
Walking in Bulgaria's National Parks
Walking in Hungary

FRANCE, BELGIUM AND LUXEMBOURG
Cathar Way
Écrins National Park
GR5 Trail
GR20: Corsica
Mont Blanc Walks
Robert Louis Stevenson Trail
Tour of the Oisans: The GR54
Tour of the Queyras
Tour of the Vanoise
Trekking in the Vosges and Jura
Vanoise Ski Touring
Walking in Provence
Walking in the Cathar Region
Walking in the Cevennes
Walking in the Dordogne
Walking in the Haute Savoie:
  Vol 1 – North
  Vol 2 – South
Walking in the Languedoc
Walking in the Tarentaise and
  Beaufortain Alps
Walking the French Gorges
Walking on Corsica
Walks in Volcano Country

FRANCE AND SPAIN
Canyoning in Southern Europe
Way of St James – France
Way of St James – Spain

GERMANY AND AUSTRIA
Germany's Romantic Road
King Ludwig Way
Klettersteig – Scrambles in
  Northern Limestone Alps
Trekking in the Stubai Alps
Trekking in the Zillertal Alps
Walking in Austria
Walking in Austria's Hohe Tauern
Walking in the Bavarian Alps

Walking in the Harz Mountains
Walking in the Salzkammergut
Walking the River Rhine Trail

HIMALAYA
Annapurna: A Trekker's Guide
Bhutan
Everest: A Trekker's Guide
Garhwal & Kumaon: A Trekker's and
  Visitor's Guide
Kangchenjunga: A Trekker's Guide
Langtang with Gosainkund and
  Helambu: A Trekker's Guide
Manaslu: A Trekker's Guide
Mount Kailash Trek

ITALY
Central Apennines of Italy
Gran Paradiso
Italian Rock
Shorter Walks in the Dolomites
Through the Italian Alps: The GTA
Trekking in the Apennines
Treks in the Dolomites
Via Ferratas of the Italian
  Dolomites:
  Vols 1 and 2
Walking in Sicily
Walking in the Central Italian Alps
Walking in the Dolomites
Walking in Tuscany

MEDITERRANEAN
High Mountains of Crete
Jordan – Walks, Treks, Caves, Climbs
  and Canyons
Mountains of Greece
The Ala Dag (Turkey)
Treks and Climbs Wadi Rum, Jordan
Walking in Malta
Western Crete

NORTH AMERICA
Grand Canyon with Bryce and Zion
  Canyons
John Muir Trail
Walking in British Columbia

THE PYRENEES
GR10 Trail: Through the
  French Pyrenees
Mountains of Andorra
Rock Climbs in the Pyrenees
Pyrenees – World's Mountain Range
  Guide
The Pyrenean Haute Route
Through the Spanish Pyrenees: GR11
Walks and Climbs in the Pyrenees

SCANDINAVIA
Pilgrim Road to Nidaros
  (St Olav's Way)
Walking in Norway

SLOVENIA, CROATIA AND MONTENEGRO
Julian Alps of Slovenia
Mountains of Montenegro
Trekking in Slovenia
Walking in Croatia

SOUTH AMERICA
Aconcagua and the Southern Andes

SPAIN AND PORTUGAL
Costa Blanca Walks:
  Vol 1 – West
  Vol 2 – East
Mountains of Central Spain
Picos de Europa
Trekking through Mallorca
Via de la Plata (Seville to Santiago)
Walking in Madeira
Walking in Mallorca
Walking in the Algarve
Walking in the Canary Islands:
  Vol 1 – West
  Vol 2 – East
Walking in the Cordillera Cantabrica
Walking in the Sierra Nevada
Walking the GR7 in Andalucia

SWITZERLAND
Alpine Pass Route
Bernese Alps
Central Switzerland
Tour of the Jungfrau Region
Walking in the Valais
Walking in Ticino
Walks in the Engadine

INTERNATIONAL CYCLING
Cycle Touring in France
Cycle Touring in Ireland
Cycle Touring in Spain
Cycle Touring in Switzerland
Cycling in the French Alps
Cycling the Canal du Midi
Cycling the River Loire – The Way
  of St Martin
Danube Cycle Way
The Grand Traverse of the Massif
  Central
Way of St James – Le Puy to Santiago

MINI GUIDES
Avalanche!
First Aid and Wilderness Medicine
Navigating with GPS
Navigation
Snow

TECHNIQUES AND EDUCATION
Book of the Bivvy
Indoor Climbing
Map and Compass
Mountain Weather
Moveable Feasts
Outdoor Photography
Rock Climbing
Snow and Ice
Sport Climbing
The Hillwalker's Guide to
  Mountaineering
The Hillwalker's Manual

For full and up-to-date information
on our ever-expanding list of guides,
please visit our website:
www.cicerone.co.uk.

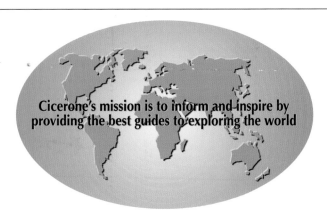

Cicerone's mission is to inform and inspire by providing the best guides to exploring the world

Since its foundation 40 years ago, Cicerone has specialised in publishing guidebooks and has built a reputation for quality and reliability. It now publishes nearly 300 guides to the major destinations for outdoor enthusiasts, including Europe, UK and the rest of the world.

Written by leading and committed specialists, Cicerone guides are recognised as the most authoritative. They are full of information, maps and illustrations so that the user can plan and complete a successful and safe trip or expedition – be it a long face climb, a walk over Lakeland fells, an alpine cycling tour, a Himalayan trek or a ramble in the countryside.

With a thorough introduction to assist planning, clear diagrams, maps and colour photographs to illustrate the terrain and route, and accurate and detailed text, Cicerone guides are designed for ease of use and access to the information.

If the facts on the ground change, or there is any aspect of a guide that you think we can improve, we are always delighted to hear from you.

Cicerone Press
2 Police Square Milnthorpe Cumbria LA7 7PY
Tel: 015395 62069 Fax: 015395 63417
info@cicerone.co.uk www.cicerone.co.uk